Tears For Fears

THE HURTING

In-depth

Laura Shenton

"Things like depression and rage are quite natural. It's just a question of getting them in context."
- Roland Orzabal, January 2014

"In the long run the depth of one's music will always be a strength as it will lead to longevity. Musical styles over the years will always change, emotions and people's connection to those emotions won't."
- Curt Smith, January 2020

Tears For Fears

THE HURTING

In-depth

Laura Shenton

WYMER
PUBLISHING
Bedford, England

First published in 2021 by Wymer Publishing
Bedford, England www.wymerpublishing.co.uk Tel: 01234 326691
Wymer Publishing is a trading name of Wymer (UK) Ltd

Print edition (fully illustrated): **ISBN: 978-1-912782-58-1**

Edited by Jerry Bloom.
Proofread by Lin White of Coinlea.

eBook formatting by Coinlea.
Printed and bound in Great Britain by
CMP, Dorset.

A catalogue record for this book is available from the British Library.

Typeset by Andy Bishop / 1016 Sarpsborg
Cover design by 1016 Sarpsborg.
Cover photo © Pictorial Press / Alamy Stock Photo.

Contents

Preface

Considering the musical impact that Tears For Fears made, particularly in the eighties, when it comes to books there hasn't been that much written about them. Whilst they have said themselves that they haven't been as prolific as other bands, it certainly isn't to say that what they have done isn't of significant merit.

The purpose of this book is to look at the music in detail. In this case, Tears For Fears' 1983 album, *The Hurting*. As author of this book, it is my aim to offer an insight into *The Hurting* in a way that discusses the music in detail in relation to what Tears For Fears' creative process was. I want to offer something factual rather than something that is peppered with my own opinion and interpretation of the music. You won't see statements in the lexicon of "this section is in the key of A and it therefore means X" or "I think this lyric means Y." For of course, the beauty of music is often in the ambiguity; it would be futile to throw a lot of my own opinions out there because it won't add anything to the literature if I do that.

It matters to present an exploration on *The Hurting* that is objective; one that embraces an extent of detail that has been put out there by Tears For Fears themselves in terms of what was intended by the album, and detail regarding how the album was perceived at the time (and beyond). As a result, throughout this book you're going to see lots of quotes from vintage articles. I think it's important to corroborate such material as there will probably come a time when it is harder to source.

The subject matter of *The Hurting* is considered by some to be pretty dark and perhaps even, uncomfortable. Good. Music

— or indeed any art form — that provokes thought surely can't be a bad thing. There is so much to say about the emotional impact of the album. Throughout this book, as much as I love *The Hurting*, I am keen to examine what it means to people universally rather than me personally. Roland Orzabal and Curt Smith have often been quite candid about the emotional relevance of *The Hurting* over the years and as such, their comments on the album will be used to inform the discussion in this book.

In the interest of transparency, I have no affiliation with Tears For Fears or with any of their associates. This book is based on extensive research and objective commentary.

Chapter One

Why *The Hurting*?

In the 1980s, Tears For Fears were a substantial band with a significant following. When two young men from Bath formed the band in 1981, there were exciting days ahead for them. By 1985, Roland Orzabal and Curt Smith had achieved global stardom through the success of their second album, *Songs From The Big Chair*. The album hosted the two memorable songs, 'Shout' and 'Everybody Wants To Rule The World'. At the height of their fame, Tears For Fears saw *Songs From The Big Chair* reach platinum status in both the UK and the US.

Whilst Tears For Fears may be best known for their second album, it was their 1983 debut, *The Hurting*, that first established their fanbase and their fame in the UK. A commercial success, the album followed the unanticipated success of their single released in September 1982, 'Mad World'. With macabre lyrics contrasted by an upbeat tempo and catchy melody, the song was stark.

As an album, *The Hurting* is fascinating in how it is largely inspired by such an unusual subject matter; the psychological traumas of childhood, depression and of course, the idea of the primal scream, as promoted by psychologist Arthur Janov. Orzabal was quoted in *The Quietus* in September 2013; "*The Hurting* was one thing: pure Janov."

It was asserted in *Melody Maker* in March 1983; "And then there's the delicate subject of primal theory. It's their main inspiration and the important lyrical ingredient of the two singles that have catapulted them to success — 'Mad World' and 'Change' — and it's the bitter core that gives *The Hurting* its painful bite. Primal theory, clearly, is their lifeblood. Very simply, it is a way of exorcising the fears picked up during childhood, by bringing out the emotions (tears) of the mature man. Nah, don't laugh, this is no opportunity press hype. Tears For Fears have resolutely stuck to their theories (it shows in all their interviews) and a quick scan of *The Hurting* lyric sheet gives you a brief introduction to the subject."

To which Smith was quoted, "The hardest thing has been not having a lot of product to back it up, and it all being an idea and it *does* sound a bit crass, us just going to the press and telling them all about it. In a sense, it sounds like a bloody ploy to get press. But now the album is coming out it will help us a lot because it will make things a lot clearer, more obvious and a lot less strange."

Orzabal: "Primal theory is a central theme to our album. You can enjoy the album for what it is. You don't have to know anything about it — all you have to know is that primal theory is incredibly human and incredibly normal. Like the album!"

It was advocated in the same *Melody Maker* feature; "*The Hurting* takes time to appreciate. The primal theory, the childishness, the wetness and the tears are an important part of the album, certainly, but what's just as important are the musical embellishments that surround the ideas — a fact that Sticks Sutherland blatantly sidestepped in his review of the album last week. There's the actual gut strength of the songs, the intricate cross fades, the dynamic melodies, the staggering use of keyboard and percussion textures (particularly the Prophet-induced marimba sound — a distinct, recognisable feature that Tears For Fears often employ). Then there are the beautiful vocals, the exquisite lyrics and the pace, dynamics and drive that have made *The Hurting* a stunning debut."

The fact alone that the well-known track, 'Mad World',

is on *The Hurting* makes it an iconic album. However, there is so much more to *The Hurting* than 'Mad World'. The distinctive drum beat and synth hook on the opening and title track is certainly memorable and it very much portrays a sense of the originality to come on what is ultimately, an engaging and unique album. Orzabal was quoted of 'The Hurting' in *Melody Maker* in March 1983; 'It's anthemic and it's a key to the album. Basically the song is questioning the way everyone feels, 'could you ease my load, could you see my pain, could you please explain — the hurting?' — it offers relief."

The Hurting is an immensely thematic album, both generally and in comparison to the Tears For Fears albums that followed. Whilst *The Hurting* wasn't Tears For Fears' biggest selling album, it was (and indeed is) a landmark album in its own right. All of the songs feature a cohesive message in the lexicon of the album's overall theme.

So is *The Hurting* a concept album? Well, that is open to interpretation, even in terms of what Tears For Fears have stipulated themselves. Over the years, there have been instances in which they have described *The Hurting* as a concept album and other instances where they have advocated that it isn't. Orzabal was quoted in *The Quietus* in September 2013; "It's a concept album. Tears For Fears was a concept. *The Hurting* is a concept album." But in response to being asked why *The Hurting* took nearly eight months to make, Smith was quoted in *Melody Maker* in March 1983; "It was such a frantic thing because we always thought our first album would be a heavy concept LP, but it hasn't turned out that way. It took a long time to even realise that it wasn't gonna be — it's all separate parts."

Either way, *The Hurting* certainly has a theme running throughout. Orzabal was quoted in *Melody Maker* in March 1983; "*The Hurting* is us from our conception up to date. It jumps about all over the place in history — the earliest songs are 'Suffer The Children' and 'Watch Me Bleed'. Later songs are

'Start Of The Breakdown', 'Ideas As Opiates' and 'Memories Fade'. It's our history. That's what we've treated it as."

A concept album or otherwise, released in March 1983, *The Hurting* made an explicit statement with regards to Tears For Fears' sound. With both Orzabal and Smith being from troubled backgrounds, the subject matters explored in the songs were certainly candid. Impressively, despite the maturity in the lyrics, Tears For Fears were still successful in managing to appeal to a young teenybopper audience too (in writing this book, I made certain to look for quotes that went beyond what Orzabal and Smith like to eat for dinner and what their favourite colours are; their music is so much more than that — nevertheless, their wide ranging appeal is certainly an achievement and indicates their success).

Orzabal was quoted in *Record Mirror* in February 1983; "Our first two singles didn't have pictures of us on the cover. We had important images and symbols on the cover because that's what we were more interested in doing — putting across symbols, instead of promoting ourselves as people. We never promoted ourselves as people because we didn't feel confident enough or good looking enough to do it… Until 'Mad World', we weren't really a pop group with an image. For a couple of weeks the record company had been saying to us, 'You might be on *Top Of The Pops* so you better get ready'. We didn't know what to do — to go on with just two of us or use the group we play with live. We didn't have a clue. We went out the same day we were on — we left rehearsals at *Top Of The Pops* and bought some clothes. Everyone chose virtually the same thing. I looked at us in the studio at *Top Of The Pops* and thought 'Bloody hell! We're a pop group!' — which was a shock. When we actually saw us on the telly I was surprised at how we looked. The first time we got on stage at *Top Of The Pops*, we just stood still and did nothing, because we didn't know what to do. I thought 'Jesus Christ we're gonna look like

Echo And The Bunnymen.' I thought, 'This is useless.' There is no way you can be so closed up and so introverted. Eventually we loosened up... 'Mad World' sold a lot of copies, far more than I imagined. We became a pop band overnight and with that comes a lot of different things."

The Hurting features the first three songs that were hits for Tears For Fears; 'Mad World', 'Change' and 'Pale Shelter' — all of which placed in the top five of the UK singles chart. In its year of release, *The Hurting* got to number one in the UK chart and remained in the listings for over a year. 'Suffer The Children', Tears For Fears' first single released in 1981, is also on the album. Some album versions of songs are different recordings to the singles that were released (there's much more on that in chapter two because the story behind each song is intriguing and the dedication and perfectionism employed by the band in the recording studio are all mini stories within themselves).

In the eighties, Tears For Fears' first two albums had the wow factor for very different reasons. Whilst it was the second album that propelled them to world fame, it was *The Hurting* that first put them on the map. A cold and dark album, *The Hurting* could be regarded as pop's answer to Joy Division's album, *Unknown Pleasures*. Comparatively, *Songs From The Big Chair* was upbeat and perhaps more explicitly commercially friendly. If anything, it all adds weight to the case that *The Hurting* was an unlikely contender in the albums chart, so much so that by the time it came to making their second album, there was plausibly an extent of pressure on the band to make songs that were less emotionally heavy. And that's what a lot of the charm is with *The Hurting*; it wasn't necessarily designed to be a happy, poppy, optimistic album and yet, there was something about it that the record buying public in the UK really latched onto.

Despite its universal and timeless message, there is a

possibility that 'Mad World' perhaps caught people's imagination on a somewhat political basis at the time it was released. With Margaret Thatcher as Prime Minister, the public's opinion was often divided when it came to what was happening in terms of society and economics. Smith was quoted of 'Mad World' in *Vice* in January 2014; "We were sitting in his (Orzabal's) flat and we were looking out of the window at people going to work, at existences we thought were pointless."

Orzabal was quoted in the liner notes of the 1999 release of *The Hurting*; "I lived above a pizza restaurant in Bath and I could look out onto the centre of the city. Not that Bath is very mad — I should have called it 'Bourgeois World'."

Smith was quoted in the same liner notes; "'Mad World' was the first single off the finished album. The intention was to gain attention from it and we'd hopefully build up a little following. We had no idea that it would become a hit. Nor did the record company."

The extent to which *The Hurting* wasn't expected to make a dent commercially was such that for Roland Orzabal and Curt Smith, they went on a dramatic journey in their careers within just a few years. Success happened quickly. They went from struggling to make ends meet whilst living in a run-down part of Bath to being one of the biggest pop groups in the world by 1985.

Orzabal was quoted in *Melody Maker* in March 1983; "I used to feel incredibly self-conscious about interviews. I used to get depressed for weeks after reading an interview, but then when you're not successful commercially, the only thing you've got to go on is critical acclaim. That's all we were interested in to start with. It was more important to get critical acclaim than to sell records. And then we *fucked* it! We started getting these *terrible* interviews which made us seem like a complete utter pair of cunts, and we thought 'God! It's not worth it!' But then 'Mad World came along and suddenly everybody started to take notice of us. Before they thought 'well these guys are fucking nutters — they're talking about this primal bloody theory business, and they're making *pop* records about it and it just doesn't all tie up'." To which Smith was quoted, "Yeah, but once we had some success, the critics started to listen to more of our music and they began to realise that it *does* tie up."

There is a lot to be said for how Tears For Fears were unafraid to embrace themes inspired by psychology and philosophy in their music. From the anguish of childhood to the struggles of entering adulthood, *The Hurting* was unapologetic in how it liberally embraced those subjects with depth and with thoughtfulness. In response to the interviewer's statement of "It's brave of you to put these views across. Most people sing songs about girls, drugs, violence and rock 'n' roll", Orzabal was quoted in *Melody Maker* in March 1983; "Well, yeah, it's kind of brave and almost foolish in a sense because of the criticism that we've had. But the songs are a natural outlet for our feelings."

Smith: "They don't have to concern other people."

Orzabal: "However, people do identify with them. They will do. I don't think that's a bad thing, because next to expressing it through song, is indentifying your feelings on a song."

Smith: "One thing we're not trying to do is preach. The fact is that that's what our songs are about, and that's about us. You can't get away from that. In a sense our songs are an introduction to primal theory."

Orzabal: "It's an incredibly difficult thing to talk about in interviews because it's so vast and covers all aspects of human nature. I'd like to suggest that people listen to the album and check it out. If they like it and are interested or identify with the lyrics, then they should read the books. The books on primal theory explain it far more than we ever could."

Both Smith and Orzabal grew up on a council estate in Bath. Whilst there are many bands whose origins and image are embedded in the concept of having grown up on a council estate, cities such as Birmingham, Liverpool and Manchester are often more associated with such an image than Bath is. It could be argued that Bath has more of an image in the lexicon of being an affluent tourist attraction; Bath isn't necessarily the first place that would spring to mind when thinking about the grit of working-class struggles.

Smith was quoted in *Medium* in January 2020; "I grew up on a council estate in Bath, which is state subsidised housing for those less fortunate. Whilst it was certainly not as rough as estates in major cities it came with the stigma of being poor and working class in an otherwise wealthy city. I don't think I ever truly cared about whether we were taken seriously or not when we started, but it became obvious over time that people found it hard to pigeonhole us. In a country that has a very pronounced class system I wasn't upper class or middle class, and I wasn't considered "hard knock" working class because I came from Bath."

Smith was quoted in *The Quietus* in 2013; "We both grew up primarily with our mothers because our fathers were absent. (My childhood) was spent growing up on a council estate, albeit in Bath, which probably has nicer council estates than some parts of the country."

Location aside, how someone feels isn't comparable to how anyone else feels. Whether it was Bath, Birmingham or Bournemouth, the fact is that both Smith and Orzabal had childhoods that came with pain and challenges that would go on to fuel their music. Orzabal was quoted in the same feature; "Curt grew up in a place called Snow Hill, and it's not so bad now, but in the early days it was not like the centre of Bath where you have all the beautiful touristy buildings. It was a block of flats. Several blocks of flats. Bath is lovely now, but it just didn't feel that way at the time."

Smith: "We had nothing, so we would go and steal things.

It was a very poor, basic upbringing, but it taught to you to be independent."

Smith was quoted in *Melody Maker* in March 1983; "We're both from broken homes. It's the kind of background where you can't ignore that there was something wrong and that's why it's more apparent in us than in a lot of people. For us, it's so obvious that we were brought up poor, that our childhood wasn't right and that's why our views on primal theory have come out."

To which Orzabal was quoted, "My dad will kill me! He's already written loads of letters to journalists telling them that what I say is untrue."

Amazing things can come from some of the most difficult situations. Orzabal said in 2013; "(My parents) ran an entertainments agency for pretty much Working Men's Clubs. We had a ventriloquist come round and he taught me ventriloquism. All the women were strippers. My mum trained strippers and was a stripper herself, and my dad used to enjoy that as well! It was very strange. We were kept out of the way while all that stuff was going on. The weirdest part of my childhood was that any guys that came round were generally guitarists and singers. So as a young kid I was exposed to people playing and singing, and my father would get out a tape recorder and record them, and sort of say, 'No that could be better', or 'You could do that again'. I grew up idolising one singer in particular, who was the antithesis of my father. Black belt at judo, big guy, sounded like Elvis. I thought, 'Yup, that's what I want to do'."

Orzabal and Smith knew each other from a young age. Smith said "Roland was kind of a nerd. He was more studious. Both his parents were very educated. Mine were definitely under-educated. So I guess, even though we grew up along the same lines, he was from a very different background. I was interested in reading — I'm interested in learning stuff, there's no question about that — from a very early stage. But on a council estate it's hard to find like-minded people. I think we were both like-minded people, but from very different backgrounds... We have a very, very similar sense of humour. Our main means of communication would be sarcasm."

In 2013 Orzabal told *The Quietus*: "I remember the first time I met Curt, he wasn't allowed out because he'd been in a fight. He'd dumped someone down the stairs. Yeah, he was a lot more rebellious."

To which Smith was quoted, "It was nothing abnormal for a council estate. Luckily I charted a path out of it. A lot of these kids went on to a life of crime. I was just trying to gain attention in whatever I could. I guess I could have gone that way, but I chose a different path. Being in a band was a legitimate way of getting attention. It didn't involve breaking the law."

Orzabal: "It's the attraction of opposites, isn't it? I never looked up to him, but I've ended up in my life with people who are more fiery than me, and bring out the fire, like my wife. I didn't marry someone timid and conservative. I guess it's one of those psychic — relating to the mind, you know? — sort of things you bring into your life, things that hopefully bring the best out in you."

Music had always been a key part of the rapport between Orzabal and Smith. Smith said in *The Quietus* in September 2013: "Roland wasn't originally from the council estate I grew up on, but he'd moved up at the age of eleven from Portsmouth, where he was from. There were two major comprehensive schools in Bath, so we weren't at the same school."

Orzabal was quoted in the same feature: "I started playing guitar, learned three chords and started writing songs. My first love, believe it or not, was country and western: Johnny Cash and a bit of Elvis. I always found myself, even if I had a group of friends — four or five people — we would end up singing and banging stuff. And I was always like a ringleader. So then, a bit later, because I was more advanced on the guitar, at school I gave guitar lessons. The guys who were learning guitar, we'd form a band, and it would go on and on like that. There were always a lot of kids who wanted to learn, and I could teach them a few things, and we'd end up being in a band. I was best friends with a guy who I taught to play bass, and he went to my school. He knew Curt from his previous school, so, when we formed our first heavy metal band at age thirteen, fourteen, we met through our bass player, Paul."

To which Smith was quoted, "They came to my flat one time and heard me singing along to a Blue Öyster Cult record, of all things, and Roland asked if I wanted to sing for their band." Orzabal: "He was playing Blue Öyster Cult's 'Then Came The Last Days Of May', and we were thinking, 'Oh yeah, maybe we've got a lead singer here.' So we were the classic Led Zeppelin format!"

The early eighties was an interesting time for pop music in terms of how drastically eclectic it was. As well as 'Mad World', a whole host of memorable singles came out in 1982; The Clash: 'Rock The Casbah', The Stranglers: 'Golden Brown' and Dexy's Midnight Runners: 'Come On Eileen'.

By early 1983, things were just as eclectic. It was advocated in the *Aberdeen Evening Express* in January 1983; "The Rolling Stones toured Britain, the first Beatles single celebrated its twentieth anniversary, the five hundredth record to reach number one was passed, and a host of new acts broke through. The pop world mourned the death of Alex Harvey while Blondie, The Jam and Squeeze all ceased to exist, and the Who quit touring. It all happened in 1982."

The underlying feature of the year in pop was the emergence of a new generation of stars who often took over the mantle from the established artists. But the likes of the Rolling Stones were still big box office. Their British tour sent a buzz of anticipation ringing through the country. After initially playing a few smaller shows, their European tour was mainly performing to rave reviews. Everyone seemed happy except Blondie who had the cheek to accuse the Stones of taking so much money out of the market, there was none left for any others to have a successful tour.

Blondie cancelled a huge European trip, but no one was really fooled. Sales of the *Hunter* album were poor, and the 'War Child' single flopped, which suggested that the Blondie bubble had all but burst. Two weeks after the tour cancellation, they split. It was the start of a series of such action from big names.

The Jam went from strength to strength in the early part of the year. 'Town Called Malice'/'Precious' had gone in at number one (the second time they had done that) and *The Gift* was acclaimed as their best album to date. But their enigmatic and controversial leader, Paul Weller, wanted to do something fresh, so the split was announced. A farewell tour was hastily arranged, and the last single, 'Beat Surrender', gave them a hat-trick of number one entries.

Meanwhile Phil Oakey's all-conquering Human League opened 1982 where they left off — on top. Both the million-selling single, 'Don't You Want Me' and the *Dare* album dominated most of January. On 1st January, only eight number ones were needed to reach the magic five hundred, thirty years after Al Martino had been first with 'Here In My Heart'. Bucks Fizz (twice), Shakin' Stevens, Kraftwerk, The Jam, Tight Fit, Goombay Dance Band and Paul McCartney and Stevie Wonder, all occupied the top spot before Nicole, a seventeen-year-old German schoolgirl, grabbed the glory. Her ballad, 'A Little Peace', also became the third Eurovision Song Contest winner in succession to reach the top.

Amidst all this the Beatles returned to the charts with a reissue of 'Love Me Do' to celebrate its twentieth anniversary. It actually reached a higher chart position than it did first time round.

Duran Duran took over the mantle of today's teen idols, while a host of new talent came to the fore as the likes of the Police, Undertones and Stiff Little Fingers struggled to make an impact. This was particularly true of the later part of the year when Wham!, Culture Club, Blancmange, Talk Talk, A Flock Of Seagulls and Tears For Fears took the industry by storm.

The landscape of pop music was tentative and uncertain in the early eighties. It comes across that there was conflict between what was being championed commercially by the music media at the time and what some of the record buying public actually wanted to engage with. As a reader letter asserted in *New Musical Express* in November 1982; "Who is the NME aiming at? The writing staff has become increasingly adventurous but their attitude has become very secular. Sometimes the paper comes over as a literary *Coronation Street*: if you miss one issue it takes weeks to catch up on the latest running joke, hip philosophies or whatever. As a music paper, your readership is limited to those interested in music and many of the broader articles are lost when they could appeal to a much wider audience. Maybe you should have a supplement for the more diverse contents or a new name. With pop being so uninspiring at the moment it would be great to see the next big change in "youth culture" free from the fickle fashions of music. Maybe the ball is rolling — how much can you help it?"

On balance though, a different reader letter that immediately followed included a statement of "The Rock Business is entertainment only. It does not change worlds or even individual thought for any length of time. So what sort of paper would we have if devoted entirely to "music"? The words themselves are fairly meaningless and you don't want endless lists of artistes' equipment or tedious "interviews" about how they get their sound. Far more interesting is what makes writers write and what it is in the world that generates song material."

It stands to reason that Tears For Fears might have been cautious about how best to deal with the press. The *Melody Maker* interviewer considered of Orzabal and Smith in March 1983; "The thought and planning of their upcoming twenty-two date nationwide tour and ultimately, the effect of months' of work on their debut LP — *The Hurting* — has left its mark. And even now, comfortably seated in the calm atmosphere of Phonogram's managing director's office, Tears For Fears can't relax. Roland and Curt are fidgety, nervous, and constantly on edge. You've only got to look at the early press assassination attempts to realise why. They are, and probably always will be, wary of the press."

In contrast to a backdrop of lots of upbeat synth pop, Tears For Fears were coming from a much darker place when it came to the subject matter of their music. Also though, there was perhaps a strong emphasis on emotional honesty overall in their work. In *New Musical Express* in November 1982, the journalist considered of Tears For Fears' lyrics that they were "an obsession with perhaps the darker, sadder elements of relationship and motive" prior to asking Orzabal, "Do you purposely eschew the investigation of love that so many chart regulars rely on?" to which Orzabal was quoted; "I think our songs are about love. Lots of people blithely sing about it without really understanding. They treat love as either romance or sex when it's not about that at all. It's letting someone be themselves. It's total honesty."

On balance, Orzabal and Smith have often advocated that Peter Gabriel and Talking Heads were strong influences. Orzabal was quoted in *Super Deluxe Edition* in March 2020; "I was always slightly obsessed with Talking Heads and David Byrne, the melodies, or lack of melodies that he used to come up with."

In *The Guardian* in December 2013 Smith said, "We'd been listening to *Remain In Light* by Talking Heads, Peter Gabriel's eponymous third album and *Scary Monsters* by David Bowie. These were amazingly produced, very rhythmic records that made us want to try something similar. Access to synthesisers gave us the chance to experiment. 'Mad World''s distinctive percussion intro was played on a Roland CR-78 drum machine. We first recorded it at twice the speed, but it sounded great slowed down."

Smith told *The Quietus* the same year, "I think there were so many influences around at that point. Gary Numan, for one. Peter Gabriel's third album. The Talking Heads record (*Remain In Light*), and (David Bowie's) *Scary Monsters*. All amazingly produced records. And so we were very aware that we wanted to get into production. And Peter's third album was probably the biggest influence on the recording, if you're going to name one. It's quite obvious in 'The Prisoner'. I actually love that song. It brings that depth to the album. I think that without 'Ideas As Opiates' and 'The Prisoner' it doesn't have the same depth."

Smith was quoted in *Vice* in January 2014; "Leading into *The Hurting*, what changed our view of music was Gary Numan." To which Orzabal was quoted, "It wasn't even so much liking him, it's that we were kids following trends and trends in those days were really powerful. You're acutely aware something is changing and then suddenly Gary Numan was number one. We were familiar with the style, having listened to Bowie, but it was a shock that he was number one."

Despite naming Peter Gabriel as an influence, Orzabal keenly asserted that his approach to making music was different to that of Gabriel's. It was considered in *New Musical Express* in November 1982; "Roland's choice of Peter Gabriel (along with Gilbert and Sullivan and Simon and Garfunkel) as a specific musical reference point prompts inquiry into the Tears For Fears production technique. Gabriel said recently it took him eighteen months to make his most recent forty-odd minutes of music and Tears For Fears are still working on an album began in July."

To which Orzabal was quoted; "Recording does take a long time. It's an urge for perfection; it only comes out right if you do it as you feel. I hope it never gets to the Gabriel stage. He tends to involve lots of other musicians and pick and choose which bits he wants while we prefer to work on our own, or just use the other members of the live group."

Tears For Fears were keen to make the best of the technology available to them. Orzabal was quoted in *Record Mirror* in February 1983; "What's come up from synthesisers should be miles ahead of any other sort of music. There will always be revivals but the future lies with electronic and digital music. Lots of the groups adopting the new technologies now are just not doing it very well. They're just poor pop bands trying to create extremely accessible music."

Smith was quoted, "I think part of the reason why everything's up in the air at the moment is that people are still finding their feet with digital and electronic music. All they're doing is making very normal music, using modern instruments. Eventually people will start to use them properly."

It wasn't always the most commercially visible musicians that Tears For Fears spoke highly of in interviews. Orzabal was quoted in *Record Mirror* in February 1983; "My favourite singles of last year were 'Shipbuilding' by Robert Wyatt and 'Buffalo Gals'. 'Shipbuilding' is so emotional and works on one level. McLaren's record works on a gut level and on a spine level. It's one of the best pieces of music I've heard recently because it's a piece of music that doesn't make me think, which is something I do a lot. The thing that's good about McLaren's record is that it isn't a song — there's no way I could play it on a guitar. I think song structure will die out. It'll take a long time because there are people trying to maintain it all the time. You can write music for the body which doesn't have to be in a song form."

Tears For Fears were not the first of musicians to embrace the work of Arthur Janov as inspiration. John Lennon had already explored Janov's ideas over a decade earlier in 1970 with his album, *John Lennon/Plastic Ono Band*. Equally, Primal Scream took their band name from a Janov book.

Although Tears For Fears were not the first to make reference to Janov in their music, the fact that they chose to do so was a big deal in terms of how they were an unknown band opting to deal with a complex and difficult subject matter as part of their debut album. Commercially, it could have been so much safer to go for something simpler and more obvious to fit in with what other synth pop bands were storming the charts with at the time.

But of course, had Tears For Fears gone for the easier choice, it is sad to think that *The Hurting* wouldn't exist. It is a challenging and unlikely album. There was certainly room for a darker style of synth pop in the charts at the time though. Tears For Fears and indeed *The Hurting* can sometimes be seen placed under the category of Goth Rock. Under such umbrella (if of course, you do choose to accept such definition) was also the likes of Ultravox, Soft Cell and Gary Numan.

Notably, as much as Janov holds a place in music history, in the field of psychology his theories have been officially discredited by the American Psychological Association. John Lennon and Yoko Ono were famous patients of his. They underwent primal therapy and there are many instances on the *John Lennon/Plastic Ono Band* album where Lennon warbles very openly on the topic of his childhood miseries. The album is considered by many to be frank and worthwhile, despite criticisms of being self indulgent.

It could be said that Lennon's album is a more significant album that refers to Janov's theories, purely on the basis that it is John Lennon and he was the first one to do it. Equally though, does that make Tears For Fears' *The Hurting* any less significant? I would argue that it doesn't. Whilst Lennon had the fame and prolific musical output behind him by the time he put out his album inspired by Janov's theories, it certainly doesn't take anything away from what Tears For Fears created and achieved with *The Hurting*.

Essentially, it could be considered that *The Hurting* is more extensive in its reference to Janov's primal therapy. Several of the song titles on the album are taken from Janov's writings. In fact, the very band name — Tears For Fears — comes from Janov's writings. Across the ten songs on *The Hurting*, each deals with subject matters relevant to emotional pain.

Orzabal and Smith forged a friendship in their teens and as a result, they grew up together with a shared understanding of where one another was coming from. Not only was this significant when it came to making *The Hurting*, but it was also an important aspect of how they developed musically to ultimately become Tears For Fears.

Prior to being Tears For Fears, Orzabal and Smith were dabbling in genres of music besides that which they ultimately became most known for. Under the band name of Graduate — their first recording band — their musical style was much closer to that of the early Beatles.

On Orzabal's eighteenth birthday, Graduate signed a record deal. Orzabal recalled, "We signed a record deal with Graduate, miraculously."

Smith: "I think we had to wait for Roland to turn eighteen. I don't think his mother was particularly happy about the whole thing. That was 1979."

Richard Zuckerman was an A&R man for Precision And Tapes Records, part of Pye Records. He signed Graduate. He was quoted in *The Quietus* in September 2013; "In about '78, '79, there was a guy called Peter Prince who ran the A&R at Pye Records, and I went and joined him as an A&R guy. Then they decided to split it into different labels, and I ran the Precision Records And Tapes (PRT) label. It was very small, just starting off, did a couple of singles and things. That was my start. There was a label called Rialto Records, and I signed them to Pye. That was The Korgis, and that's what led me down to Bath. I think they were friends with Roland and Curt's band, Graduate. I went down and saw them in a club, and, for me, Roland in particular was the guy. Roland's best friend was Curt, and then they had the other guys around the band, but Roland was the absolute star. He was the everything of the band. I'm a bit of a player myself, and when I used to hang with Roland the thing that struck me was the way he played the guitar, and the way he wrote songs. I couldn't even discuss chords with him: he had open tuning, and his chord structures were bizarre and unbelievably weird. So I checked them out, and they had a little local following, and that was enough to know that I should get involved."

Graduate was a five-piece, sharp suit wearing, mod revival band. In 1980, they released an album called *Acting My Age*. It featured a single called 'Elvis Should Play Ska'. The single did well in Spain, but in Britain it didn't even get into the top one hundred. The Elvis referred to in the single's title was Costello, not Presley, but all the same, it didn't commercially make a dent in a way that was desirable for Graduate.

Orzabal recalled in 2013: "I suppose we (Graduate) weren't a particularly serious group, and we were very, very much down the food chain when it comes to the authentic groups like The Specials and Madness and that kind of stuff. We weren't very good. But we had a little bit of radio success in Spain, which was my first experience of hysteria and girls hanging outside the hotel... Previous to that I'd been unemployed. My wife had been working three jobs in bars and restaurants, and I got my first PRS cheque and I thought, 'That's a good job!'"

Richard Zuckerman added, "The marketing was pretty bad.

I just brought the single back from the UK, and I'm looking at the packaging and, erm, it's pathetic! If you look carefully, the faces are just cut-outs! And that's the sleeve! The thing about Pye was, by the time you got to the seventies, they were always known for being a singles company. They sold masses of things like 'The Birdy Song' and Lena Martell's 'One Day At A Time' and things like that. I mean, millions and millions of singles! But we could never sell any albums. Certainly I don't remember much being done about Graduate's album."

Regarding the inspiration behind naming the band Graduate, Smith was quoted in *Medium* in January 2020; "The name really came from Simon and Garfunkel more than the movie. Although in retrospect, was it to do with teenagers trying to navigate an adult world? Your guess is as good as mine. Leaving the band was a part of that, I think. We always had the desire and belief that music should be deeper than playing live. The other band members were very into the tour life and the immediate gratification that brought, I think we were looking for something more."

It was in 1980 that Orzabal and Smith split from Graduate. Thirty-three years later Smith said, "The upside of Graduate is that we learned that we were not made for travelling in minivans." Richard Zuckerman added, "We did a little British mini tour, and they had a tour bus, and I followed them around in my car. I remember Roland sneaking away from the tour bus, and I drove him round the back streets of Newcastle — or somewhere, I can't remember — and we were having a good old laugh. I think Curt was quite miffed that I took Roland and left Curt on the bus!"

Smith: "Yeah, we learned a lot of things. And it was also an interesting time, because around then technology had just started taking off, in the sense that Linn drum machines and the need for a band really didn't exist any more. Before then it was always kind of bands based around the studio, but Gary Numan changed all that. And we realised we wanted to concentrate on making really good records, something that lasts."

Orzabal: "We went to the record company, Precision, and we told Richard Zuckerman that we had split and we were going to do synth pop. And he was like, 'Great, okay'."

Orzabal was quoted in *The Guardian* in December 2013; "We'd been in this mod band called Graduate, but Gary Numan had shocked us out of all that. He was getting number ones wearing black eyeliner, and there we were doing knees-ups to Madness. So we split from the band. I got an asymmetrical hairstyle, Curt got plaits, and we started listening to synthesiser music."

On 21st May 1981, Roland Orzabal penned a letter to Richard Zuckerman:

"Dear Richard,

Please find enclosed the aforementioned biography for Tears For Fears. Any additions or corrections will be welcomed.

Yours,

Roland

Tears For Fears are from Bath and consist of two songwriters: Curt Smith and Roland Orzabal, plus help. They call their music "affects music", using the relationships between people and moreover those within the family, as the main source for their themes. They regard this subject as being of far more importance than that of "politics" or "fashion" which appear to be the current trend in popular music today.

They see Tears For Fears as being a serious but loose

arrangement and hope to tap the reservoir of local talent which is abundant in the area.

Curt and Roland, who are both nineteen, had been playing together in several outfits over the past four years, but due to their disillusionment with the so-called "democratic" way under which groups operate, decided to form Tears For Fears and were soon signed by PRT.

Their debut single 'Suffer The Children' was recorded in Bath and produced by David Lord, who, apart from producing the Korgis' hit 'Everybody's Got To Learn Sometime' is currently working with Peter Gabriel on his fourth album."

Zuckerman asserted that he was more interested in working with Roland Orzabal than he was in working with Curt Smith. Zuckerman told *The Quietus* in September 2013: "I had no problem with (Graduate) breaking up because for me it was always Roland. I don't want to diss Curt too much, but they were friends. There's no doubt that Roland was helping Curt along. He helped him to learn how to play bass guitar and gave him a job in the band. But it was all about Roland. Roland was the star."

Although Zuckerman is important in getting Orzabal's and Smith's career off the ground, it is worth considering that in many interviews, Orzabal has advocated for the fact that he worked well with Smith on *The Hurting* because they were on the same page in terms of what it was that they wanted to create.

When it comes to working effectively in any creative industry, such rapport is incredibly valuable. In such regard, I advocate that both Smith and Orzabal were equally important figures when it came to making *The Hurting*. Orzabal is the only credited writer on *The Hurting*, but as he said of Smith in *Vice* in January 2014; "He was seriously my partner-in-crime.

He couldn't articulate himself musically like I could, but we were of one mind. We had the same feelings then, which we probably don't now."

Smith told *The Guardian* in December 2013; "'Mad World' was easy for me to sing because I could relate to Roland's lyrics. We were both the middle of three sons and had been brought up by single mothers with absent fathers. My father always worked away, and died when I was seventeen, but I hated him by that point. It hit me later in life, but back then I was teenage and angry. The song was the perfect platform. It worked better with my voice because it's more melancholic, darker."

Although *The Hurting* itself was something of a commercial gamble on the basis of its mood and subject matter, when forming Tears For Fears, Orzabal and Smith were forward thinking enough to come to the conclusion that they needed to work on developing a sound that was more likely to resonate with a British audience.

By the early eighties, the British music scene was already past the initial injection and excitement of the punk movement. Still though, Orzabal considered that there was room for heavy subject matters in the mainstream. He was quoted in *Vice* in January 2014; "I wasn't a massive Joy Division fan, but they were one of the few bands contemplating feelings of suicide."

As with any artists' musical development, it is typically not the case that they go from one point to the next straight away; creativity is often a more fluid process. As part of this, when Tears For Fears released 'Suffer The Children', their first single in 1981, there was a very different feel to the song compared to how it was recorded for its inclusion on *The Hurting*. The 1981 single release of 'Suffer The Children' could plausibly be regarded as having a slight folk music feel to it — certainly in comparison to the album version of the song anyway.

When *The Hurting* was released in March 1983, Tears For Fears were an unknown entity. When it came to the charts, they were in eclectic company but certainly amongst artists whose song subjects could be considered more palatable, or at least, light-hearted; Wham! Duran Duran, Spandau Ballet, Simon Le Bon etc.

It was considered in *Record Mirror* in February 1983; "Tears For Fears' success is unlike that of their double named contemporaries. Hard work, live work and a steady nurturing of support preceded their success. Fashion designers, makeup artists and expensive producers did not propel Tears For Fears into the charts. This is why Tears For Fears are the only one of a clutch of bright new pop groups who might just provide something worthwhile... Tears For Fears will carry on working in their quiet unassuming way. They may make great pop, they may not. But they'll follow their calling with a deal more dignity than most of their contemporaries."

It was considered in *New Musical Express* in November 1982; "In what must be one of the most surprising chart surges of 1982, Tears For Fears have carried the weighty mantle of post-Joy Division music to the top, capturing the elusive markets of screaming teenies and the heavy overcoat brigade on the way. 'Mad World', like much of the group's other material, is the epitome of a "grower", an insidiously simple tune aided, in no small way, by the championing of John Peel and Peter Power. Friends since childhood, Roland Orzabal and Curt Smith, the mainstays of the group, grew up in Bath where their musical dabblings led to a stint in Graduate, a contrived group that rapidly dated as the first flush of the revival petered out. It did, however, provide them with the money and facilities to work together on their own material which they managed to place with apparent ease, with Phonogram Records. A couple of releases put out without particular backup, compounded by a somewhat lackadaisical approach, left Tears For Fears beached — bereft of an audience, a manager, a firm contract or even some sort of game plan. Although not enamoured with the prospect of gigging, they tested the water with a support slot on The Thompson Twins' desperate We're Pop Stars tour."

Orzabal said in 2013; "I think we were cool for five minutes until we went on *Top Of The Pops*, really. John Peel was playing us — we did sessions for John Peel when nobody had really seen us — but then if you're signed to a major label, two young pretty boys, they're going to push you into doing the poster pop as well, and at that point you're going to lose a lot of people."

It didn't take long before Tears For Fears' tour dates were being keenly anticipated. It was advocated in the *Aberdeen Evening Express* in March 1983; "The early rise to the top for Tears For Fears almost came too quickly for a duo who are now one of pop's hottest properties. For when Phonogram Records first expressed an interest in Curt Smith and Roland Orzabal, they only had two songs completed in their set. But that was enough to convince Dave Bates — discoverer of The Teardrop Explodes, Monsoon and Trio among others — that they had what it takes to succeed. His faith was soon justified when 'Mad World', only the third single, became one of the best-selling discs of 1982. Now they are set on their first major tour, taking in the Capitol, Aberdeen tomorrow. Curt and Roland became friends when they met at school in Bath, and it was there they developed the smooth melodies to accompany the heart-beat percussion which grabbed the attention of the record-buying public. It was one of the original numbers, 'Suffer The Children', out as a single, which brought some ripples of interest, and the follow-up, 'Pale Shelter', went on to become a great favourite on the club circuit. 'Mad World' was expected to go a similar way, only achieving moderate sales, but the band were staggered when it hit the top five just before Christmas. Despite that success, they were reluctant to tour, but were persuaded to compile a backing group for what became a hugely successful tour with the Thompson Twins. From there it was back to the studio to make the debut album under the capable production of Chris Hughes, renowned for work with Adam And The Ants. The resultant offering is *The Hurting*, which carries versions of both early singles as well as 'Mad World' and an extended version of the current hit, 'Change'. *The Hurting* may not attain classic status, but it has to be remembered it is the debut album of a band who hitherto lack experience. The best from Tears For Fears is yet to come, for sure."

The Hurting is full of catchy melodic hooks. As far as eighties music goes, it feels vital to stipulate that it has eighties written all over it and in such regard, it certainly doesn't stick out like a sore thumb in the same way that it does thematically.

As well as sounding "of its time" though, emotionally, it offers so much in terms of its potential to strike a chord with anyone who has ever felt depressed; anyone who has ever felt an overbearing desperation to escape from the prison of their own emotions. *The Hurting* is a powerful album no matter which way you look at it.

Ultimately, it would be so easy to overlook some vital aspects of *The Hurting* and that's why telling the story behind it is warranted; a new and relatively unknown band made an album about the traumas of childhood and it stormed straight to the top of the UK album chart. There's something pretty damn special about that.

Chapter Two

The Making of *The Hurting*

Many names came and went in making the singles prior to Orzabal and Smith working on *The Hurting*. By the time it came to recording the album, as Orzabal said decades later; "It was just the four of us who were responsible for it: myself, Curt, Chris Hughes and Ross Cullum. And we were living in London. Our homes were Bath."

And of course, in terms of the band's overall image, it has always been centred around the nucleus of just Roland Orzabal and Curt Smith. Orzabal was quoted in *Record Mirror* in November 1982; "We keep Tears For Fears as a nucleus of two because that's how it started. We do use regular people though. We acquired drummer Manny Elias who's been with us ever since and then Ian, whom we bounce ideas off. Live, we're augmented to a five piece by Andy Davis, who's from local group, Slow Twitch Fibres."

It was reported in *Melody Maker* in March 1983; "Tears For Fears use additional musicians on stage. They call on a reliable team of seasoned pros, who they claim, take orders from them, not vice versa. If you thought that Curt and Roland are simply pretty puppets fronting strong session men, think again. A quick phone call to Andy Davis (late of Stackridge, currently with Slow Twitch Fibres and part of Tears For Fears' live back-up team) reveals that Roland comes up with all the keyboard parts. Davis simply follows the instructions. Further evidence comes during a long discussion with the duo which emphasises their knowledge, love and passion for musical equipment. Roland's favourite current synth is the simplistic Emulator ('it'll become an incredibly popular pop instrument — we've just started to use it in the studio'), they've both toyed with Peter Gabriel's fave — the much more complicated Fairlight — and the duo earnestly keep abreast of all new musical equipment developments... Ultimately, both of them want more control, principally in the production of their material." To which Smith was quoted, "I personally think we'll be ready to produce our next album. Whether we'll be allowed to or not is a different matter."

Orzabal was quoted in the *Shropshire Star* in January 2018; "It's never been easy for us. We didn't go in and record *The Hurting* in two weeks, like the Beatles did with their first album. We took ten months to a year. It's always been our fate almost to have to work really hard, with nose to the grindstone, to get anything out. That's partly our own fussiness. It's also that we attract fussy people. Then it's a democracy of fussiness and that makes it hard work. Our output hasn't been phenomenal. But that's no bad thing because we haven't bashed people over the head with our presence. That's why a lot of people are very glad when we do surface."

Orzabal was quoted in 2020; "When I wrote *The Hurting* it was largely in my flat in Bath above a pizza place, with an acoustic guitar; I was the bedroom guitarist, the bedroom strummer. I think Caroline at the time was working two or three jobs, so I was on my own for large portions of time, or even Curt would come around and we'd have a cup of tea and we'd talk about music, and I'd be actually writing, as he reminded me the other day, with him in the room, almost sonically picking his brain. I remember when he went to see (Bristol band) Electric Guitars support the Thompson Twins, when they were a seven piece, before they became a trio. And it was all this highly percussive, Talking Heads-inspired music and he described to me what it was, and I came up with a song that was in that mould, that's called 'The Hurting'. That's the way our relationship was then, and I think as a young man I was a sponge for everything. My antenna was incredibly powerful. And I was depressed without a doubt. And I had all these things going on; moving away from home and into a relationship, being faced with the threat of adulthood."

'Suffer The Children' was written and sung by Roland Orzabal. It was Tears For Fears' first single, released in November 1981. It was recorded not long after Graduate had split. The original single version of the song was produced by David Lord. It was recorded at his own studio in Bath, Crescent Studios. Orzabal said in September 2013: "Richard (Zuckerman) funded our first recording with David Lord. We did that song, and we used the Graduate drummer, Andy, on it."

Smith was quoted in the liner notes of the 1999 release of *The Hurting*: "'Suffer The Children' was the first song we did together when we left Graduate. It was our very first experimentation with sequencers and drum machines, with a guy called David Lord, who worked with Peter Gabriel and different people down in Bath. So that was actually the first song we did as Tears For Fears."

'Suffer The Children', along with 'Pale Shelter', were the two demo songs that resulted in Tears For Fears getting a record deal with Phonogram in 1981. Smith said 2013; "Myself and Roland went up to London with, I think, just two songs to play to A&R people. We had well produced demos, which I think were just 'Suffer The Children' and 'Pale Shelter'."

Orzabal: "From the Graduate deal, we had a relationship with a production company with Tony Hatch, composer of the *Crossroads* theme tune (and who had written songs for many Pye artists). He'd actually co-produced our (Graduate) album. He had a son called Darren, and we gave Darren the demo tape of 'Suffer The Children' and 'Pale Shelter'. 'Pale Shelter' we did at Ian's. We had a photo session done as well. Darren saw all the majors, but we had only two bits of interest. One was from Charlie Ayres at A&M, who was very nice, and the other was Dave Bates. And that was only because Darren had walked in, played it, I think Dave Bates had grunted, and Darren Hatch was halfway down the corridor when Dave ran after him. So by such thin threads we managed to get interest from Dave."

Dave Bates had joined Phonogram as an A&R talent scout in 1976. He had already signed Dalek I Love You, Def Leppard and The Teardrop Explodes prior to signing Tears For Fears. In 2013 he said; "I don't believe it was (Tony Hatch's) son. It was a chap called Les Burgess. He was a song plugger from the publishing company. On that day he brought six cassettes of songs. Def Leppard was self-sufficient and wouldn't use MOR (middle of the road) songs in a million years. The Teardrop Explodes equally so. I thanked Les and said goodbye for another six months. After he had gone I thought about one of the cassettes I had heard, one in the middle of the pile. I called Les up and asked him about them. He told me they were two young guys, twenty years old, who lived in Bath. I told him I wasn't interested in the songs, but the duo: could they be an act? I travelled down to Bath to meet them and remix two of the songs to see if they could be singles. I had never heard Graduate. After a couple of meetings they told me about the band. They didn't want to play me anything. So I had to go out and get a copy of the single. The sleeve gave a clue as to what it was going to be like... Hearing the first songs of Tears For Fears gave me hope that I could get hits with this synth band. I liked both of the boys a lot. Roland was a little moody and reserved, but sharp as a tack, with great humour, while Curt was the affable chappie who was really interested in his career and how to succeed."

Orzabal said in 2013: "I think the advance was about £12,000, which for us was, like, 'Woah!' It might have been £14,000, but it was a two single deal."

There was certainly work to do though. Dave Bates was quoted: "I'd tried very hard to sign Depeche Mode, offered them a big deal, but was rebuffed. Depeche were very pop orientated; Soft Cell was an odd mixture of pop and a dark suggestion. Ultravox, Visage and Spandau Ballet were the new romantics and were already established and successful. Tears were more of an intellectual, moody proposition. I was allowed to sign them on a two-single deal, with an option for an album, which means I had to succeed in the charts with the singles before being allowed to carry on and make an album. I released 'Suffer The Children', and John Peel picked up on it and compared them to Joy Division. The NME reviewed it and likened them to Joy Division as well."

A considerably different recording of 'Suffer The Children' features on *The Hurting*. That version was re-recorded and was produced by Chris Hughes and Ross Cullum. The album version is without the vocals sung by Curt Smith that feature at the beginning of the single version. Both versions of the song include vocals by Orzabal's wife, Caroline, during the bridge.

When 'Suffer The Children' was released in the UK in 1981, the twelve inch version featured a remix and an instrumental version on the A-side. On the B-side of both the seven and twelve inch versions was a song called 'Wino'. On 'Wino', there is a notable absence of synthesisers; in terms of Tears For Fears' sound overall at the time, it is an unusual track and somewhat a little out of character. Whilst the 'Suffer The Children' single was championed by Radio One DJs John Peel and Peter Powell, it didn't chart. Orzabal said in 2013; "The first single was played for about six weeks on Peter Powell alone."

'Suffer The Children' was reviewed in *Smash Hits* in November 1981: "Dippy boys in OMD-ish (Orchestral Manoeuvres In The Dark) jumpers with a sluggish message song enlivened by overpowering vocal noises currently mistaken for singing. Generous lashings of melody though and I like their style, despite the fact that one of them is called Roland Orzabal."

With Tears For Fears being a predominantly unknown entity in 1981, there wasn't quite enough commercial power behind their name to give the initial release of 'Suffer The Children' the push that it needed to succeed. However, the success of the 1985 album, *Songs From The Big Chair*, was such that Phonogram reissued the single: The audio content was exactly the same but there was a variation to the art on the picture sleeve. The 1985 release of 'Suffer The Children' did better commercially; it charted just shy of the top fifty in the UK.

Whilst 'Suffer The Children' is significant in terms of how it was Tears For Fears' first single, and indeed part of the original demo that helped land them their record deal with Phonogram, it was small fry in the grand scheme of things compared to the commercial successes that would follow. A video was never produced for the song and all three original single versions, along with 'Wino', were not released on CD until 2013 as part of the thirtieth anniversary reissue of *The Hurting*.

In terms of the personnel changes that occurred after first version of 'Suffer The Children', Orzabal told *The Quietus* in September 2013; "Richard Zuckerman either got the sack or he resigned for another job. I don't know. But what he did was let us go with the master tapes. So we had 'Suffer The Children'." To which Zuckerman was quoted, "They were slowly cutting it back, and eventually there was no real record company left. They weren't signing acts any more, and I left to go into music publishing."

Smith: "We then luckily met a guy called Ian Stanley. He was kind of a rich kid who had been working with the old members of Graduate, and the old members of Graduate were talking me up, so he was interested and offered us the chance to record on his eight track at home."

Orzabal was happier with the version of 'Suffer The Children' on *The Hurting* than the first version that they did as a single. He was quoted of 'Suffer The Children' in *Melody Maker* in March 1983; "That's how it started for us. That was the first thing we ever did together. It's been remixed in a more basic, less flowery way than the original single."

'Pale Shelter' was written by Orzabal and sung by Smith. It was released as Tears For Fears' second single in early 1982. The song was originally titled 'Pale Shelter (You Don't Give Me Love)'. At the time of its initial UK release, the song failed to chart.

Although the first version of 'Pale Shelter' didn't have much success commercially, the version of the song that was re-recorded for *The Hurting* was released as a single. It was the third song to be released from *The Hurting* that placed in the top five of the UK chart.

In terms of how it was written, 'Pale Shelter' started off as a sequence of two chords that Orzabal had been mulling over on the acoustic guitar for a number of weeks. It seems that a relaxed environment was the most constructive for creativity. Orzabal was quoted in *Record Mirror* in November 1982: "When I'm not touring I like to stay at home and go over my groundwork. I set everything up in the living room and experiment, which drives my wife mad. I'll play my guitar and hope the songs will come... I've never forced myself to write a song because if you do that you find yourself repeating earlier themes. My songs are inspired because I wait for them to come. I wouldn't say I write a lot of songs because I'm very fussy. I do get a lot of ideas, but I only pursue a few. Nor do I put my ideas on to tape or on to paper. What I do is sing it over and over again until it's firmly locked into my head and then I'll start thinking about lyrics. Sometimes I've finished a song but I've learned to leave it alone for a couple of weeks in such cases... For our second single, 'Pale Shelter', I kept playing two chords for weeks and weeks, then one morning I woke up and sang the tune and the words, just like that. Then another day I was flicking through an art book and came across *Pale Shelter Scene* by Henry Moore, so that wrapped everything up nicely." Henry Moore's 1941 artwork, *Pale Shelter Scene*, is a painting of people taking shelter in an underground station in London during the second world war.

Orzabal said, "Ian Stanley's studio was a godsend because there was access to a synthesiser and a drum machine. To actually sit at home with just an acoustic guitar was tough." He was quoted in *Record Mirror* in November 1982: "I've written pretty much all of our stuff up until now. If we do complete songs then they're written on the guitar, but if we're just working on fragments of tunes they'll be written on keyboards... One of our keyboard players, Ian Stanley, has a twenty-four track studio in his house so we like to work there. It's nice because we can demo and write there, and also take a break and wander round the rest of the house. We spend a lot of time mucking about with gadgets and computers. I'm not too fond of working in the studio because the pressure is dreadful. I like working on my own writing the songs and I enjoy recording the songs in demo stages, but when it comes to making the finished article, the music industry pressure almost becomes too much to bear. When it gets to the mastering stage and you have three days to finish three songs, there is no way you can feel creative. It's entirely the opposite, totally destructive. When we're at Ian's there's no sense of being trapped. That's why we prefer to work in Bath."

After Tears For Fears' had released 'Suffer The Children' the first time around, it was decided that 'Pale Shelter' would be their second single on the basis that it sounded more commercial. There were practical reasons behind this decision too though; David Lord was busy working with Peter Gabriel

(Smith was quoted in 2013; "David Lord went on to produce Peter Gabriel's fourth album, and had produced a band called The Korgis, who'd had a couple of hits.").

Mike Howlett was brought in to produce as a result of this. Orzabal and Smith didn't have a good working relationship with Howlett. In particular, they considered that his use of Linn drums was excessive and they didn't work with Howlett again. Curt Smith was quoted in the liner notes of the thirtieth anniversary release of *The Hurting*; "Mike was far too commercial for us. I don't think we felt we were learning anything and we're not good at being pushed in a direction we don't wish to go."

Dave Bates; "There was some enthusiasm, but not enough to get going. They were not a live act, so nobody could "discover" them. Their lyrics were deep, maybe even dark. They had meaning, not the usual pop fare. So single number one went down. Then 'Pale Shelter' came out. Again little nibbles, but no bite. So I tried using Mike Howlett, who'd produced Orchestral Manoeuvres In The Dark."

When 'Pale Shelter' was re-recorded for *The Hurting* with the production by Chris Hughes and Ross Cullum, a brief piano lick was added to the arrangement. "We did about four tracks. It was not going the way Curt and I had intended, so we alerted Dave Bates and that was stopped," recalled Orzabal in 2013. "We then had a meeting in Bath with Chris Hughes. We knew him from an album by a band called Dalek I Love You."

Bates; "I had been involved with Dalek I Love You, who were an influential band to British synthesiser acts. They were from Liverpool and originally featured Andy McCluskey, who went on to form Orchestral Manoeuvres, Dave Balfe, who was in Teardrop Explodes, Budgie, who became the drummer for Siouxsie And The Banshees, Dave Hughes, who also was in Orchestral Manoeuvres, and Alan Gill, who went on to join the Teardrop Explodes as well. I loved synth music and artists, and for some inexplicable reason 'Dalek I' never made it."

In the early days, who would produce for Tears For Fears in the long run remained a tentative subject. Orzabal was quoted in *New Musical Express* in November 1982; "Producers tend to dissipate the energy in production. We'll probably produce the second album ourselves but we're getting on alright with Chris Hughes for this one."

The feeling of needing to get things just right perhaps added extra pressure. "I would never really choose to record like that again. *The Hurting* was painfully slow," said Orzabal.

Smith: "I'm not sure that it was weak decision making on anyone's part, more a sense of, 'This isn't good enough, perhaps we could try this instead'."

Orzabal told *Melody Maker* in March 1983: "We've re-done 'The Prisoner' monstrously. It's so much better than the way we did it before (on the B-side of 'Pale Shelter')." Smith chimed in with, "It's just so weird, and it's great that it comes after 'Change'."

Orzabal: "It's like A-level punk! It's got so much guts, and as the choir screams, there's a fade with reverb and then you get the marimbas which signal 'The Start Of The Breakdown', the last track on the album. In a sense, we've said *The Hurting* is the start of the breakdown, but that's far too cryptic!"

It was reported in the same *Melody Maker* feature; "Another reason for the album's delay was the problem they had finding a suitable producer. They experimented with various people (including Mike Howlett) before settling on Chris Hughes, noted for his work with Adam Ant and Dalek I Love You. Under Hughes' guidance, Tears For Fears stripped down a lot of songs, starting a few of them again from scratch. The reassessment shows. Much blood, sweat and toil has gone into *The Hurting*."

In more recent times Smith has said, "We were learning along the way. The band we had before, Graduate, was very much a live band, and when we recorded we just went in the studio and played live. It wasn't layering and producing. This was us learning how to layer and produce, and trying to find our own voice with other people around us pulling us in different directions. So the process of learning in that scenario made it kind of difficult."

In November 1982 Orzabal told *Record Mirror*: "Most of the time we tend to be in the studio, and basically I'm in there working from morning until night. We've been having quite a lot of problems in finishing off our first album, so we're working very hard."

Then of course, there were all the other things that needed juggling. Dave Bates recalled, "The stress was because we had a single taking off, TV shows to do, radio sessions, press, photo shoots, more interviews. Each single took three months to line up with artwork, manufacturing, video, advertising campaign, long lead magazines et cetera. The recording was going slow because the people involved were perfectionists. They were taking demos and making them better with more ideas going into them. Writing songs in the studio is never a good idea."

Perhaps it was simply the case that building a working rapport within any team takes time. Orzabal was quoted in *Super Deluxe Edition* in March 2020: "Ian (Stanley) was really there from the beginning, he was the guy who offered us the time and the place to record. And then he was squeezed out of *The Hurting*, not for any particular reason and certainly there was no malice. But, yeah, I think Ian provided this huge bridge between the artist — which was Curt and I — and Chris Hughes. So, we had a very, very strong chain of command, right from the lowly artist up to the record company. So, we had us, then Ian, and then Chris — and their relationship was amazing at the time — and then Chris was a good friend of Dave Bates, the A&R man for Polygram. So, that's, you know, the communication within that chain of command was excellent... *The Hurting*; that was a painful record to make. There was so much attention to detail and deliberating over hi-hat velocity."

The version of 'Pale Shelter' released in 1982 was available as a seven inch and a twelve inch single. The twelve inch features an extended version of the song. The B-sides of both formats contains the song, 'The Prisoner'. It is a brash and strongly electronic piece, inspired by 'Intruder' by Peter Gabriel, which showcased liberal use of sampling and synthesisers. As with 'Pale Shelter', 'The Prisoner' was also re-recorded for *The Hurting*. Even though the 1982 single release of 'Pale Shelter' garnered some attention in the US for club play, it went largely unnoticed in the UK.

It was in 1983 after the success of the singles 'Mad World' and 'Change' that the re-recorded version of 'Pale Shelter' was issued as a single. Available as both seven and twelve inch singles, there were eleven different variations of the single made available for purchase, some of which were coloured vinyl and picture discs — a popular marketing gimmick throughout the seventies and early eighties. In all cases, the track on the B-side was called 'We Are Broken', which is actually an early version of the song, 'Broken' that later featured on *Songs From The Big Chair*.

In combination with proactive promotion and Tears For Fears becoming a bigger name as they toured throughout the UK, the 1983 release of 'Pale Shelter' saw a single release of the song finally become a chart success as it got to number five in the UK. Orzabal's wife, Caroline, sketched the cover artwork for the 1983 release of the 'Pale Shelter' single.

When 'Pale Shelter' was reissued in the UK in 1985, it was within the top seventy-five in the singles chart. The 1985 release of the single featured the same track listings as the original 1982 release.

The promotional video for 'Pale Shelter' was made in early 1983 in Los Angeles. It was directed by Steve Barton. The video includes a range of unusual imagery — an alligator in a swimming pool and a police officer directing traffic. A notable scene in the video is an imprint of a large iron on a runway at Los Angeles International Airport. There is steam coming off the tarmac that Smith and Orzabal walk on. There is another scene where the duo stroll into a sea of flying paper aeroplanes. One of the planes hits Orzabal in the eye. The scenes in the video are iconic to the extent that they have been included as part of several Tears For Fears video collections. 1983's *Videosingles* and 1992's *Tears Roll Down (Greatest Hits 82-92)* are just a couple of examples of this.

Smith said of 'Mad World', "Dave convinced the label to let us make the album, and the third single — the first one from *The Hurting* sessions to be released — was 'Mad World'." Bates: "If I was going down, I was going down having done everything I could to make this successful."

Orzabal told *The Guardian* in December 2013: "There was a group around called Dalek I Love You. One of their lyrics went something like 'I believe the world's gone mad' which summed up my feelings of alienation from the rat race. I had suffered from depression in my childhood. My dad had been in the second world war, had electric shock treatment, suffered from anxiety and was abusive to my mum. I kept a lid on my feelings at school but, when I was eighteen, dropped out of everything and couldn't even be bothered to get out of bed. I poured all this into the song."

Orzabal originally wrote 'Mad World' on the acoustic guitar. In the same *Guardian* feature he said, "I wrote it when I was nineteen, on the dole in Bath. We're known as a synthesiser group, but back then I just had an acoustic guitar. I've not told many people this, but I was listening to Radio One on this tinny radio and Duran Duran's 'Girls On Film' came on. I just thought 'I'm going to have a crack at something like that.' I did and ended up with 'Mad World'. It sounded pretty awful on guitar though, with just me singing. However, we were fortunate enough to be given an opportunity by Ian Stanley to go to his very big house and muck about on his synthesiser. Ian became our keyboard player and he had a drum machine too. All we needed was someone who knew how to work it. Eventually, we made the first demo of 'Mad World' still with me singing. But I didn't like it. So I said to Curt, 'look, you sing it.' And suddenly it sounded fabulous."

Smith; "Normally it's pretty obvious. If it's a softer song it's normally me. If it requires being belted, it's normally Roland. My voice is a lot darker, a lot more melancholic, and Roland is more of a shouter. He's trying to make a point. Which is very loud. So those are the differences in our voices, basically. 'Mad World' and 'Pale Shelter' and 'Change', even though they're pop songs, wanted to be more melancholic and softer, and that's my voice. 'Mad World' seemed to come pretty naturally, and it was the beginning of our relationship with Chris and Ross Cullum. They brought a lot to the process, and we were really enjoying working with people who knew what they were doing. And also it's a very simple song, and we wanted to make it sound different, and the only way to treat the song was in the production, and we agreed on all the production on that track. So in that sense it was enjoyable."

Orzabal: "I was very particular abut the songs I wanted to sing, and if I could use my voice. We did 'Mad World' with Chris (Hughes) and Ross (Cullum, engineer). It was just brilliant. Had it continued like that it would have been amazing! The recording of 'Mad World' is so warm, so atmospheric. I'd made the demo pretty much on my own. The way that Chris augmented it is fantastic. It's a very earthy sounding record."

Hughes: "We did it at Britannia Row Studios in London. Roland had a vision of how the song should sound and feel, and they both had a strong sense of what they wanted. The small team of Orzabal, Smith, Hughes and Cullum set about quickly re-recording an already well defined 'demo' and turning it into the track we all know."

'Mad World' was initially intended to be the B-side of the first release of the 'Pale Shelter' single in 1982. However, the record company were convinced that 'Mad World' had the potential to be a single in its own right.

Orzabal: "It did start out as a B-side because it was a song that I wasn't totally enamoured with. I'd tried singing it. We needed a B-side to 'Pale Shelter'. I took it in to play to Dave Bates and he said, 'No. That's way too good for a B-side. You've got to keep it.' I said, 'okay, sure.' And it was really Dave that said, 'No, that's the next single'." To which Smith was quoted; "We argued about that the same way we argued with the American company about releasing 'Everybody Wants To Rule The World'. We're not A&R people! We didn't expect 'Mad World' to be a hit." Orzabal: "We thought 'Suffer The Children', 'Pale Shelter' maybe…"

Other songs were considered for their potential as a single before 'Mad World' was chosen. Smith was quoted of 'Mad World' in *Vice* in January 2014; "We thought it was a really great, original track but we also thought there were songs on the album that were far more commercial. So we thought we'd release it first and that it would garner us some critical acclaim because it was interesting and different."

A year earlier Smith recalled, "(Dave and I) actually believed that it was the coolest sounding thing on the album because it was very, very different. But it's pretty dark. The reason we released it was that we felt it would give us credibility. I always thought it would just take time. I honestly felt the quality was there. It was just a question of finding the right breakthrough. There were times of concern after we'd released two singles and neither was a success. Polygram had signed us for just two singles initially, and those were 'Suffer The Children' and 'Pale Shelter'. But Dave had a belief in us. We had a belief in ourselves. Chris Hughes was then on board as a producer. And we thought we were an album band, not a singles band. Especially with *The Hurting*."

In *New Musical Express* in November 1982 Orzabal said of 'Mad World'; "I'm completely surprised, I just don't know who's buying it. We had the support from the DJs who've been playing our stuff for some time, but the way all the other DJs picked it up immediately was totally unexpected."

Thirty years later his thoughts were pretty much the same; "I couldn't believe it! It just kept going up the charts in those days where records didn't just go in at number one and fall. It was quite remarkable! It was a muted excitement because we were still making *The Hurting*, but every week *Music Week* would come out: 'Oh yeah, you've gone up ten places.' Just incredible! Who knew?! It's bizarre!"

Dave Bates said, "Slowly but surely the record took off on radio. The video was getting used too. Then it took on a life of its own... 'Mad World' went to number three."

The video for 'Mad World' was filmed in the grounds of a country house in late summer 1982. The video was directed by Clive Richardson who was already known for his work with Depeche Mode. It was the band's first music video and features a pained looking Curt Smith staring out of a window. There is a small scene in the video of a party. Friends and family of Tears For Fears, including Smith's mother and his wife Lynne, were part of the cast for this scene. Smith told *The Guardian* in December 2013; "It is a dark song but it brings back happy memories. When we made the video in a country estate on the cheap, we bussed all our friends and family up from Bath and had a fun day. The woman who's having the birthday party in the video is my mum."

In another scene, Orzabal can be seen dancing outside near a lake. Dave Bates said in 2013; "I wanted to make a video for it. In the recording studio Roland used to do this dance when he was enjoying himself. I had never seen anyone dance this way: odd, weird, unique. Perfect for the video, some odd plot of being able to see the world from a different view through a window. He did this dance of his in the video, which became very eye-catching."

Smith: "It was nothing peculiar to me. This is what Roland does in the studio: he's constantly doing weird dance moves. And we thought, 'Why not put it in the video as well, because it's interesting?' I was certainly not embarrassed by it, put it that way."

In *The Guardian* article of December 2013 Orzabal said, "I'd come up with this dance for it and used to do it a lot in the studio, so the record company told me I had to do it in the video, since Curt was singing and there was nothing else for me to do. So there I was, stuck by this lake doing my flying wombat impersonation, but it worked."

In an interview for *Melody Maker* in March 1983 Orzabal said, "Everybody knows this one ('Mad World'), but we haven't remixed it because we were so happy with it. There's a gap between 'The Hurting' and 'Mad World', but at the end of 'Mad World' the tambourine fades as the intro of 'Pale Shelter' sucks up. It's a total cross fade. You see, the tracks on the whole of the first side, apart from the first track, run totally into each other. At the end of 'Pale Shelter' it comes to an abrupt halt and immediately snaps into 'Ideas As Opiates'."

Orzabal said of 'Ideas As Opiates' in the liner notes of the 1999 release of *The Hurting*; "That's the chapter from Janov, and it's really a reference to people's mindsets, the way that the ego can suppress so much nasty information about oneself — the gentle way that the mind can fool oneself into thinking everything is great."

Smith was quoted of the song in the same liner notes; "It really was all about that kind of thing — the psychological answer to religion being the opiate of the masses, whereas we thought ideas were, more than anything else."

'Ideas As Opiates' was the B-side of 'Mad World'. On the twelve-inch release of 'Mad World', a mix called 'Saxophones As Opiates' was also featured on the B-side. Orzabal said of 'Ideas As Opiates' in *Melody Maker* in March 1983; "It's a sub-section in a Janov book. I saw that heading and I thought 'Jesus! What a brilliant title!' and immediately the same moment I came up with the verse. Basically it's about ideas and beliefs. Things like religion actually produce opiates in the brain. Things like endorphins, which can be a thousand times stronger than morphine. These, Janov says — I sound like a fucking Communist don't I? — actually help repress pain, because they're drugs. That's what the song's about. People believe things because it makes it easier for themselves."

To which Smith added, "It'll help you in the sense that it'll make it easier, but it won't help you in any real way."

Orzabal: "Yeah, it's like people believe in God because it makes them feel better, even though there's no rational explanation for it. Basically, you can say *anything*, because I find you will always think those things and those thoughts make it easier for you, and 'lies spread on lies', because they *are* lies! It's a new version of ideas by the way (a much meatier re-mix from its original setting on the B-side of 'Mad World') and it throws everything. 'Ideas As Opiates' actually fades on the last chord as the wobble into 'Memories Fade' fades up, so it's like totally related and flows incredibly well on the first side."

Orzabal was quoted of 'Memories Fade' in the same feature; "It's fairly self-explanatory. Memories fade but the scars still linger. Memories of bad experiences will fade and disappear, but the scars and how it's affected you will always stay with you. Again, it's another sad song, which is why it's so good after 'Ideas As Opiates' because it makes it *worse*!" To which Smith responded, "That's the stage where everybody goes through the window!"

'Change' was Tears For Fears' fourth single release. After 'Mad World', it was the second song that features on *The Hurting* to get into the top five. Released in early 1983 and following on from the success of 'Mad World', 'Change' also resulted in Tears For Fears having some success in the US where it got into the Billboard Hot One Hundred in August 1983.

Orzabal said in *The Quietus* in September 2013; "I wrote 'Change' for my wife to sing. We made a demo. And Curt heard it and said, 'That's a good song.' I said, 'Really?'"

Smith said of 'Change' in *Melody Maker* in March 1983; "It justified its release (as a single) in the sense that it went into the charts, but it wasn't our personal choice." Upon being asked by the interviewer, "Does the album lose its momentum here for you then?", Smith replied, "Yeah. The good thing about that is that 'The Prisoner' comes up directly after 'Change' and that really fucks it up!"

Dave Bates said in *The Quietus* thirty years on; "There was demand for the next single to be lined up. But it would mean more interruptions to the recording process, with interviews, video shoot, artwork et cetera to be done for it in advance and during the release. 'Change' was perfect as a follow up." As with 'Mad World', Clive Richardson directed the video for 'Change'.

It was certainly a busy time for all concerned. It was reported in *Record Mirror* in February 1983; "Tears For Fears go out on the road for their biggest tour ever in March. The group, who have just released their new single, 'Change', will also have their first album out around the same time as the tour. Three extra musicians — two keyboard players and a drummer — have been drafted in to join the duo."

On the B-side of 'Change' is a song called 'The Conflict'. It is one of the few Tears For Fears songs where Curt Smith shares a writing credit with Roland Orzabal. The seven-inch version of 'Change' is the same mix of the song that features on *The Hurting*, but it is in a slightly edited form. The twelve-inch single of 'Change' showcases an extended remix of the song as the lead track. Whilst many copies of the twelve-inch single features the seven-inch mix of the song as one of the B-sides, some feature an altogether different recording. Ironically, this mix is labelled the "New Version" on the UK cassette release of *The Hurting*, where it was included as a bonus track. This bonus track has a different set of lyrics and it actually predates the seven-inch mix.

Confusing stuff! But then, it is plausibly reflective of how keen Orzabal and Smith were to get things just right; they didn't seem reluctant in doing new recordings and new versions of their songs for the purpose of improving them and for being able to execute their ideas in a way that did them justice.

Upon being asked, "Isn't 'Change' a disappointing follow up to 'Mad World'?", Orzabal was quoted in *Record Mirror* in February 1983; "It's a song we're not particularly happy with. It didn't come out the way we wanted it. We wanted it to be a bit more vibrant. The DJ at our local disco won't play the twelve-inch of 'Change'. Still, we've re-recorded it for the album."

The songs on *The Hurting* that were released as singles have a strong pop element to them musically but much of the more introspective material are the tracks that weren't released as singles. For instance, 'Ideas As Opiates' has a very minimalistic sounding beat and expressive melismatic vocals. The track could be regarded as being more artistically experimental than the songs that were released as singles.

'Watch Me Bleed' has a very indie music feel to it (way before the term was even coined in the mainstream!). Equally the saxophone on 'Memories Fade' has something of a wailing quality to it.

Essentially, there are some very eclectic moments on *The Hurting* in contrast to the songs released as singles. More so, some of the album-only songs are thematically important to the overall feel of the album. Orzabal was quoted of 'Watch Me Bleed' in *Melody Maker* in March 1983; "It is virtually a reiteration of 'Memories Fade' in an uptempo state. It was actually written before; I consider 'Memories Fade' as the final statement, but 'Watch Me Bleed' reiterates it on the album."

***

Orzabal and Smith both had unhappy childhoods. Smith's parents separated when he was young and in a bid to get the attention he craved, he indulged in a range of petty crimes. The problem came to a head when he was arrested for stealing cameras from his school. Orzabal urged Smith to read Arthur Janov's *Primal Scream*. In *The Quietus* in September 2013 Orzabal said, "I had a guitar teacher, and she introduced me to a book called *The Primal Scream* (by Arthur Janov). And I read it, and it became my bible. The theory is called The Tabula Rasa theory, or the Blank Slate theory. A child is born a blank slate, and then all the terrible things that happen to it — the childhood trauma and the rejection, not enough love — become suppressed and then turn up as neurosis in later life. The therapist would try to lead you to recall something that happened to you, and your way of mourning — and it's a deep way of mourning — is that you actually cry. Not as an adult, but actually in a sense you're going really, really deep."

To which Smith responded, "It's not a novel idea. I just think Janov explained it in better terms than most people."

Orzabal: "I converted Curt, you might say. I suppose both of us were believing we were victims, so we would quite often try and convince other people of the validity of Janov's ideas... I suppose we were the only two. You know what it's like when people have a specific belief and they don't have any room for anyone else's beliefs: it's a turn off. And I was definitely one of those… I was one of those people in school who used to work hard and then, when I was about seventeen, eighteen, I had a mental Copernican inversion, so instead of just following what I was being told and doing really well and getting A's, I just started questioning everything. We were reading a lot of existentialism, both in French and in English, so that kind of set me off." To which Smith added, "Those teenage years when you're looking for all the answers…"

It was Arthur Janov's 1980 book, *Prisoners Of Pain*, that largely inspired some of the lyrical content on *The Hurting*. Further to this, the very name of Tears For Fears comes from Janov's work. Smith said; "Once I'd got the name Tears For Fears in my head, which was from the Arthur Janov book, *Prisoners Of Pain*, I told Roland. I think pretty much straight away we knew that was going to be the name… The record company didn't think we should call ourselves Tears For Fears because they'd had The Teardrop Explodes, but we were pretty adamant. And my argument back then was it's like arguing with the Beatles about their name. I mean, what a lame name! But once the music's out, who gives a shit? Led Zeppelin, you know? These things become iconic once you make music."

Smith was quoted in *Radio & Records* in August 1985; "A lot of people thought our first album was really negative — whereas it was us, really, not explaining ourselves well. Our idea wasn't 'things are bad but never mind.' Our idea was 'things are bad so let's do something about it' but people don't get that."

Orzabal said, "I never even felt there was negativity. It was reflectiveness. Having said that though, I don't think it was ultimately communicative. And I think now, this stuff is reaching out more."

The Primal Scream, Primal Therapy: The Cure For Neurosis (the full title of the book) was first released in 1970. In the book, Janov described what he experienced with the patients he was treating over the months that he was developing primal therapy. In 1967, he worked with sixty-three patients over a period of eighteen months, during which he urged them to scream about the things that had hurt them in their childhoods. Janov claimed that his method resulted in a one hundred per cent cure rate.

The Primal Scream is reported to have sold over one million copies globally. It was read by tens of thousands of people in the US alone. In his 1988 book, *The Lives Of John Lennon*, author Albert Goldman asserted that Janov sent pre-publication copies of *The Primal Scream* to a number of famous people including Mick Jagger as well as John Lennon. It wasn't long after this that Lennon underwent primal therapy with Janov. As well as John Lennon, other famous advocates of primal therapy included actor James Earl Jones and pianist Roger Williams.

The success of *The Primal Scream* was such that it raised Janov's profile to that of a celebrity. His fame and success served as inspiration to many therapists who, despite not having met him, started to offer programs in a similar vein. Even though Janov's work was liberally questioned by some of his peers in the field of psychology, the book, and indeed the therapy it advocated in favour of, was popular.

The popularity of Janov's work at the time could also have been in the fact that its approach was universally relatable; he offered a wide ranging definition of neurosis, stating that it begins for most people in early life and can exist as a result of anything from more isolated traumatic events to neglect and abuse on a day to day basis. According to Janov, neurosis could therefore begin at birth from the result of that in itself being a difficult experience.

Janov's idea that feelings from childhood are suppressed in a way that results in adult neurosis is something that both Smith and Orzabal strongly identified with. Orzabal was quoted in *Rolling Stone* in June 1985; "I rushed out to everybody I knew and started blubbering to them about it. Everybody thought I was a nutter. The only person who could see any sense in it was Curt."

According to Janov, primal therapy is a trauma-based therapy on the basis that neurosis is caused by the repressed pain from trauma in a person's childhood. Janov advocated that the repressed pain can be brought forward to a patient's conscious awareness in order for a resolution to be achieved from re-living particular events and fully acknowledging and expressing the pain during the therapy. By recalling and re-enacting a specific past event — usually one from early in their life — a patient is empowered to express the repressed anger and frustration. The patient, under the guidance of the therapist, is encouraged to express their feelings via unrestricted and random screaming, hysteria or violence. Essentially, Janov and those who advocated in favour of the therapy deemed it to be cathartic and thus, constructive.

Janov advocated that primal therapy could be more constructive than talking therapy on the basis that talking therapy is based on a higher level of reasoning in the patient's brain and it doesn't fully allow them to access the source of their pain on a more basic and foundational level.

Primal therapy enables a patient to re-experience the things that caused them pain in their childhood. It is intended to be objective and direct rather than something that requires a patient to analyse their pain. The purpose of this is to reduce or eliminate the trauma a person carries with them from early life that can colour how they feel and behave as an adult.

Janov considered that pain in and of itself doesn't hurt because, as soon as the person goes into it, it becomes simply feeling. Most of the suffering is in the blockage or repression, not the pain itself.

Smith said in *Medium* in January 2020; "The perceived difference between adulthood and childhood, to me, if there is one, is acceptance. I'm not convinced we grow out of any of those feelings. With knowledge, we just learn to accept them for what they are and hopefully integrate them into our everyday lives without judgement".

Janov believed that a lot of the pain a person experiences in childhood exists as a result of needs going unmet. He advocated in his book, *The New Primal Scream* in 1992; "Our first needs are solely physical ones for nourishment, safety and comfort. Later we have emotional needs for affection, understanding and respect for our feelings. Finally, intellectual needs to know and to understand emerge."

Janov asserted that when needs go unfulfilled for too long, pain is the result. There is a strong emphasis on the importance of getting needs fulfilled throughout Janov's work. In *Prisoners Of Pain*, he stated that "Need is a total state of the human being — and at birth we are almost nothing but need."

He argued that from as early as being a helpless newborn baby, survival is at stake in nearly every second of a person's existence. Orzabal was quoted in *Vice* in January 2014; "We believed we were victims and that very much coloured our approach to *The Hurting*, thinking that we were born neutral beings and that our tough upbringing troubled us."

In *Prisoners Of Pain*, Janov elaborated on his earlier point about childhood: "Primal pain is deprivation or injury which threatens the developing child. A parent's warning is not necessarily a primal pain for the child. An infant left to cry it out in the crib is in pain... It is not hurt as such which defines primal pain but rather the context of the hurt or its meaning to the impressionable developing consciousness of the child."

Orzabal was quoted in the liner notes of the 1999 release of *The Hurting*; "We were really big on this at the time — we really thought children were born innocent and good and holy... When you've got kids of your own, you realise how bloody difficult it is. But it's that kind of thing — saying look at what you're doing with your child." He was quoted of 'Pale

Shelter' in the same liner notes; "It's a kind of a love song, though more referring to one's parents than to a girl."

In recent years, the popularity of primal therapy has declined. A reason for this could be in how many of Janov's peers were not satisfied that he had managed to demonstrate outcomes of his work extensively enough for them to be convinced of its effectiveness. Further to this, some have advocated that not only was Janov's treatment ineffective, but harmful. There are still therapists who practice primal therapy today but it is something done more on the fringes than in the mainstream of psychology.

Orzabal told *The Quietus*, "Curt and I are both the middle of three boys, and in my situation there was domestic violence. There are a lot of people who have difficult childhoods. My childhood was the same as my two brothers' and they didn't go around moaning about it! We can all make a big deal that we were council estate kids. But that was the biggest thing that upset me, that my dad would be physically violent towards my mum. And it got so bad that in the end she left."

Many of the songs on *The Hurting* are pretty upbeat musically but the vibrancy of 'Pale Shelter', 'Mad World' and 'Change' are such that the painful lyrics should not be overlooked. In *Vice* in January 2014 Orzabal said, "You have songs that work almost regardless of the lyric. 'Pale Shelter', if you analyse it lyrically, is sensitive and emotional. But live, it's so up-tempo. There's a real dichotomy. It's the same with 'Mad World'."

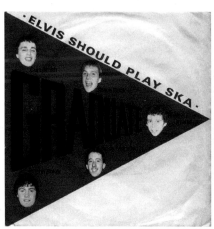
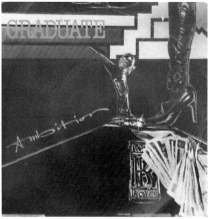

Roland and Curt tasted their first success with Graduate.
Mad One b/w Somebody Put Out The Fire was the first single
with two tracks recorded before the album: A rare and highly
sought after item for Tears for Fears fans. The album, *Acting
My Age* spurned other singles including Elvis Should Play
Ska b/w Julie Julie.
Ambition b/w Bad Dream was the band's last single release
and although the B-side was from the album the A-side
wasn't.

The most familiar album cover with the boy was released in most countries, but some territories opted for a different design with a photo of Roland and Curt by a lake with ducks in it. This was initially used for several territories including North America, Brazil, Italy and Germany, as well as Japan, where it came with the usual obi strip, with information about the album in Japanese.

Mexico

Netherlands

There were a few variations on the cover art of the cassette releases.

USA

Canada

The alternative cover was replaced on later reissues of the album.

1989

The compact disc was still in its infancy when *The Hurting* was released in 1983. As is commonplace, the Japanese have reissued the album on CD several times, each with a different obi strip.

2001

2015

1981

1982

1985

1985

Tears For Fears' first two singles were recorded and released before The Hurting. They were re-recorded for the album and these versions were reissued later.

UK

USA

UK

Japan

Mad World was the band's third single and the first to hit the charts, peaking at No. 3 in the UK. It was released in a multitude of different formats including a double single version.

Change was the follow up and reached No. 4 in the UK. It was also the band's first US entry.

As a mark of the album's popularity a 30th anniversary 4-disc box set was released in 2013. As well as a remastered version of the original album it includes a disc of b-sides and remixes; a CD of radio sessions and a DVD of the 1984 concert film In My Mind's Eye, in which the band perform The Hurting live at the Hammersmith Odeon (almost in its entirety). The package was completed with a replica tour programme and a 34-page hardback book.

Chapter Three

Impact And Legacy

There is nothing reserved about *The Hurting*. It is unapologetic in how it avoids so many songwriting clichés. Whilst it could have been easier from a commercial perspective to avoid dealing with the subjects of psychology and depression in the lyrics, Tears For Fears took what could be considered as a risk. It paid off.

Smith told *The Quietus* in September 2013: "To be honest, *The Hurting* was kind of an uphill struggle. Because it wasn't your average pop record: Myself and Roland spent a lot of time trying to make it an artistic record, even though it definitely had melodic tunes on it. We wanted the album to have some meaning, and a lot of the time that goes counter to the way record companies think. So at times it was an uphill battle, but gratifying when it became successful, because we realised you could do both: you could be artistic and successful."

The lyrics of 'Watch Me Bleed' are brave. Whether they are a cry for help or more antagonistic in their approach, they are certainly stark and memorable. *The Hurting* is full of gut punching moments where lyrically, the album is very attention grabbing. On 'Suffer The Children', the lyrics explicitly convey, and indeed question, "the pain of birth". Considering the relatively young ages of the two men behind the album, the boldness of their lyrical exploration is perhaps all the more impressive in context.

So was *The Hurting* wise beyond Orzabal's and Smith's years? Quite possibly. That said, it feels important not to negate the merits of their work — or indeed overestimate those merits — purely on the basis that Tears For Fears were young men when they created an album full of deeply explored dark themes. No matter how you look at it, 'Mad World' is as effective, direct and stunningly melodic as it is angst-ridden and heart-wrenching. Both musically and thematically, the song has so much going for it that it's hardly surprising that it has been covered a number of times by other artists, and across a range of musical genres too; heavy metal, folk and techno to name just a few. Memorable examples that spring to mind include covers by Lily Allen, Jasmine Thompson and Twenty One Pilots.

In *The Guardian* in December 2013 Smith said, "We released 'Mad World' as a single because we felt the music press would like it. But it was also supposed to just give us a foothold for the next two singles, which were more commercial. We didn't expect it to become a hit. All sorts of people have covered it. Gary Jules sang 'enlarging your world' at one bit, but the correct lyric is actually 'Halargian world'. Producer Chris Hughes had a running joke in the studio about this made-up planet and a catchphrase: 'Oh, that's so Halargian.' I put it in the song, and it sounded right."

Smith stated on his official website in 2010; "With 'Mad World''s again-resurgent popularity, I'm getting asked more frequently about the last line on the album version from *The Hurting*, a line which I occasionally also sing in concert. The actual line is: 'Halargian world.' (Not 'illogical world', 'raunchy young world', 'enlarging your world', or a number of other interesting if not amusing guesses.) The real story: Halarge was an imaginary planet invented by either Chris Hughes or Ross Cullum during the recording of *The Hurting*. I added it as a joke during the lead vocal session, and we kept it. And there you have it."

Dave Bates said in 2013: "Let's take a simple view: a

hit song has to have a catchy chorus, something anyone and everyone can hum, whistle or sing while at work, driving or walking. 'Mad World' had that. A vocal that is unique, stands out and is easily identified? 'Mad World' had that. Then a production or sound that has something uniquely identifiable that stands out? 'Mad World' had that. From the first time I heard it, I believed that it was a hit."

Orzabal was quoted of 'Mad World' in *Vice* in January 2014; "If you analyse the chorus, it's two notes."

The previous year Orzabal said of 'Mad World': "That song, God bless it, has done so well, with other people covering it as well. When I heard the Gary Jules version, I was just gobsmacked. I thought, 'Woah, blimey! Well done! Well done, nineteen-year-old self, you!' It's just one of those records. I think it was the sound which was bang on. At the time it was progressive electronic music. There were barely any guitars. It had that slight heavy beat to it, and I think it's probably the best vocals Curt's ever done."

Smith: "Obviously there's stuff I've done on my own that I think is better, only because they have more meaning to me in the sense that I wrote the songs. But yeah: I think it's one of the best ones I've done."

To some extent, *The Hurting* seems to be driven by a theme of exasperation in terms of, what a person wants isn't necessarily what they can have, no matter how much they yearn for it. As much as the lyrics of 'Pale Shelter' convey what is lacking emotionally from a parent, there is also a line that states "all I want to be is completely in command." Well, you can't have it both ways. The way in which *The Hurting* seems to acknowledge that is incredibly powerful and intense. And indeed, 'The Prisoner', despite the harrowing lyrics, is a damn good melody that is immediately memorable. It's such a juxtaposition and yet, it works.

Lyrical and emotional appraisal aside, *The Hurting* is an

important album because in the context of early to mid eighties music, it fully utilises an effective balance between a range of instrumentation, both electronic and more conventional: synths and the various methods associated with such (for instance, sampling) as well as guitars and drums. Whilst Orzabal and Smith took influence from groups who were commercially at the top of their game in the early eighties, they were also interested in the more musically complex sounds of Peter Gabriel's early solo work.

This influence is evident, perhaps, in the atmospheric keyboard sound and almost tribal drum pattern that both feature on 'Start Of The Breakdown'. The same could be said of the marimba sound that contributes to the instrumental hook in 'Change'. As unique as it is, *The Hurting* still makes use of a multitude of features that were typically characteristic of early to mid eighties pop music.

Thanks to producers Chris Hughes and Ross Cullum, gated drums and even saxophone sounds make an appearance on *The Hurting*. In addition to this, despite their heavy subject matter, 'Mad World' and 'Suffer The Children' are melodically memorable to the extent that when played live, they have choruses that audiences often sing along to. In this regard, it stands to reason that both songs were commercially successful as singles, even in view of the fact that 'Suffer The Children' didn't quote grab the record buying public the first time around of its release.

The overall sound of *The Hurting* clearly marks it as an album made in the UK in the early eighties. Whilst some may consider the lyrics to be draining, musically it has a lot of playback value. It is memorable. It sounds very much of its time and yet it is still iconic for the unusual quirks that it offered in comparison to what else was going on with pop music at the time.

Smith was quoted in *Medium* in January 2020; "Those that

feel nostalgic for past musical eras tend to forget all the bad or average music that was also prevalent then. It's because only the music with some depth lives on. There's plenty around now if you choose to look, and that will be the music that lives on in future decades. The rest will be forgotten."

When *The Hurting* was released, it received mixed reviews. In March 1983, it was considered in *Smash Hits* that "there's no doubting the talent on display." In the same month, the review from *New Musical Express* was more scathing: "This record and others like it are a terrible, useless sort of art that makes self pity and futility a commercial proposition... Tears For Fears and their listeners sound like they've given up completely, retreating from the practical world into a fantasy... Just the sort of doom-laden dross you'd expect from the lyrics: rehashed and reheated hollow doom with a bit of Ultravox here, diluted Joy Division poured everywhere, and the title track sounding suspiciously like one of the old pompous outfits with a welter of mellotrons — Barclay James Harvest per chance?"

Also in March 1983, it was considered in *Melody Maker* that "Tears For Fears' pop primal therapy tends to luxuriate in the attention it attracts, sounds ironically happy to wallow inspirationally instead of seeking exorcism... The Tears For Fears formula — to translate childhood traumas into adult romance with Freudian fanaticism — is ludicrously laboured but, crucially, their lyrical lethargy is salvaged by what really sells them; their structural invention... sensibly, their suffering's usually controlled to sound smooth... The success of *The Hurting* lies in its lack of friction, in its safety and, for all their claims that coping with relationships has been warped beyond their ken, Tears For Fears have contrived an assured masterpiece of seduction."

The album was reviewed in the *Reading Evening Post* in March 1983; "Tears For Fears are no synthesiser posers. Their debut reveals rich talents. Curt and Roland have had one big hit with 'Mad World' but there are more in store on *The Hurting*. This bodes well for the duo's tour."

The Hurting was reviewed in *Rolling Stone* in July 1983; "Britain's Tears For Fears stand out among the current crop of identikit synth-pop groups by virtue of their resourceful, stylish songwriting and fetching rhythmic sway. Granted, the adolescent angst and bleak, pained romanticism of singer-instrumentalists Curt Smith and Roland Orzabal sometimes come off as an adequate imitation of Joy Division, at best. But for every lapse into sackcloth-and-ashes anguish on *The Hurting*, the duo's debut album, there is a heady, danceable pop tune like 'Change'. On that track, a breathless core riff and nervous percussion accelerate the song's strong disco pulse. And on both 'Mad World' and 'Pale Shelter', beguiling hooks and panoramic guitar effects suck the listener into dizzy whirlpools of cleverly synthesised orchestration. 'Start Of The Breakdown' is a successful venture into artier territory, a macabre play-by-play of emotional collapse that's heightened by the stark contrast of exotic percussion flourishes and a bleak, descending keyboard motif. Tears For Fears may be too concerned with their own petty traumas, but it is a testimony to their refined pop instincts that they manage to produce this much pleasure from the pain."

The Hurting was reviewed in *Musician* in November 1983 as "an artful compromise between pure electronics and classic pop instrumentation, blending slick synthesiser gimmickry with hypnotic staccato guitar effects and sensitive piano figures." It was advocated in the same review that the lyrics made Tears For Fears seem too "obsessed with their own troubled youth, dissecting with almost masochistic glee their sundered romances and smallest psychological tremors like transistorised James Taylors and Jackson Brownes."

With the mixed reviews in mind, Smith was quoted in *The Quietus* in September 2013; "People never understood or got to grips with Tears For Fears, because it's not the norm. I think the fact that people have never been able to put us in a musical genre or a musical bag has been confusing."

Mixed reviews aside, *The Hurting* sold well and the three singles spawned by the album that reached the top five in the UK were popular dance club tracks.

A performance that took place at Chippenham Goldiggers was reviewed in *Melody Maker* in March 1983; "It's a serious business, life. Tears For Fears take themselves and their music seriously, and demand that others do the same: well, I'll try. There's no time or space for glamour or gimmicks on this stage, except the band's favourite stance in silhouette. They let the mics provide the atmosphere and the songs speak for themselves; no fancy dress or makeup, no cheery chat or posing — the authors of this music are more intent on examining the sinister aspects of the human condition and bemoaning fate. They'd become known as the Leonard Cohen of the eighties if they didn't happen to be talented enough to couch their despising lyrics in alluring and arresting songs. The line-up is simple enough: keyboards, drums and keyboards at the back. Curt Smith and Roland Orzabal at the front. Curt is the public image, the video face, of Tears For Fears but in fact he only takes the lead on a couple of songs. 'Mad World' is his moment, but it's Roland of the heavy jowls who sings most of the numbers, possibly because he's got a more distinctive voice, but probably because he wrote more of the material. What makes them so good, these arresting and alluring songs, is the careful planning of the structure on each one. The attention to detail and the precise sequence of instrumental interplay that come to a peak in a song like 'Pale Shelter' approaches the intellectual beauty of Joy Division or U2. What makes them so bad are examples like 'The Way You Are', featuring a synth quietly screaming its head off, the odd rhythmic inconsistency, and choruses that can be best described as a primal wail. It's painful really — pass the paracetamol. Tonight was their first-ever major headlining gig, and while it didn't fall flat, nobody was screaming in the aisles. This might change after umpteen sets, but essentially Tears For Fears are bound to feel uncomfortable on stage because their music is made to listen to, not to dance to; theirs are private experiences that ask for a private hearing. I'm reminded of Marvin — here we are, brains the size of planets. Don't ignore Tears For Fears, they're not going to go away yet, but don't expect to be starstruck either."

It does stand to reason that the overall sound on *The Hurting*, upbeat singles aside, didn't necessarily lend itself to the kind of live music experience that the reviewer may have been hoping for. I suggest that the review is perhaps reflective of the way in which as an album, *The Hurting* resonated very strongly with some people and not at all with others.

A performance was reviewed in the *Aberdeen Evening Express* in March 1983; "Whatever happened to value for money as a consideration of bands on tour? It certainly isn't something uppermost in the minds of Tears For Fears. The duo, Roland Orzabal and Curt Smith, came to Aberdeen with a hugely successful album in their set, and nothing else. In all, this amounted to just over forty-five minutes on stage, and even the very best don't get away with that. *The Hurting* is a very good album. Tears For Fears are a very good band, with the potential to be great, but blatant pawn-offs like this are a sure fire way to lose fans. What concert there was, was tight, punchy and occasionally inspired. Surely they could have taken time out to prepare themselves properly with a set of real depth to do their undoubted talents justice."

It clearly took a bit of time for Tears For Fears to embrace the demands of performing over being in the studio. Smith was quoted in *Smash Hits* in 1983; "The very first moment I stepped on stage, I'd had it. My hands got all sweaty, I could feel my heart pumping, the adrenalin flowing and I was so uptight. I really thought it would eventually go away but I still have it. I'm not a very pleasant person to talk to before I go on. When we played The Lyceum in London recently I was so nervous about the audience reaction I decided the only thing to do was abuse them. I remember shouting out 'this is for those of you who are just too cool to clap' before we did 'Mad World'. I think that helped me enjoy the show, because I was telling them what I really thought. I always look very serious on stage and one night, when I was with my old band, Graduate, I remember noticing this girl in front of me pulling her mouth apart with her fingers, making faces in an attempt to make me laugh. She succeeded and I met her afterwards. She's now my wife Lynne."

On balance, it is plausible that Tears For Fears were great on stage and that it was the reviewers who were being disparaging because they weren't comfortable or used to what Tears For Fears and their music were about.

Orzabal was quoted in *Melody Maker* in March 1983; "It's far easier live to project the emotion. I think we're more gutsy live, I love it! When you do certain gigs well, you walk off stage and you feel like you've just had sex!"

Reviews are always subjective. Tears For Fears first gig took place at Moles Café in Bath in May '82 and was reviewed by a journalist by the name of Johnny Waller (the date and publication of the review is unknown — that's newspaper clippings for you!): "Love. The losing, the finding, the hoping, the hurting. Tears For Fears are about love, and it really doesn't matter whether you choose to laugh in their faces or open your heart. Love may feel sorrow and shed tears, but it never goes away. After two striking, swooning singles, Tears For Fears are playing their first ever gig, and, in their innocence, in their naïve trust, laying themselves wide open to cynical sneers and macho ridicule. I think of their ethereal live show as a palace of passion, where they stand naked and vulnerable, yet safe in their own self-belief and determination. Tears For Fears are a welcome re-statement of caring, comforting devotion, with just the merest hint of sexuality. Musically, Tears For Fears are a swirling, dancing, swooping concoction of synthesiser backing, while Curt and Roland play bass and guitar respectively, also taking care of all vocals, switching and dovetailing like a West Country Hall And Oates. And the songs! Well, melodies like the heartache of 'I Can't Get To Sleep', the sweeping OMD lushness of 'Suffer The Children' and the yearning plea of 'The Hurting' are destined surely to end up on an album of immeasurable class and appeal. As commercial as either Teardrop or Spandau, but without either of those band's excessive pretentiousness. Listen to the 12" version of 'Pale Shelter' (recently single of the week in *Sounds*) and prepare to welcome Tears For Fears out of a wilderness bounded by geography and emotion. They are a baby's cry, a lover's plea."

Over three decades later, *The Hurting* is arguably a representative milestone in eighties pop. Compared at the time to music from the likes of Joy Division and Echo And The Bunnymen, the album stands out as memorable and relevant. Orzabal said in 2013; "I think Joy Division and Echo And The Bunnymen, the bands that wore black, allowed the sort of 'Woe Is Me' bleak songs that we were doing. We had a new romantic spin in terms of that was the way to have the hair at the time — asymmetric, or plaits or whatever — but we weren't anything like Duran Duran. You'd see them on a yacht and it was all about excess and glamour. We weren't about that. It was all about an interior world, and not about the exterior world." To which Dave Bates added, "They were never a Joy Divison. Miles from it."

The Hurting got the ball rolling for Tears For Fears and by 1985 they were at the height of their global commercial success with *Songs From The Big Chair*. Orzabal was quoted in *Smash Hits* in 1985; "What we're doing now is a lot of people's dream, but it's never been a dream for us. It's good, the success, and it's justified, but I don't care about maintaining it. Even though I know we could, if we set our minds to it, be the biggest band in the world."

In 1989, they released their third album, *The Seeds Of Love*, before splitting up and each doing some solo work. Smith was quoted in *The Sun* in November 2017; "We've had lots of ups and downs but we know that the things we do separately are not as great as the sum of what we do together."

Songs From The Big Chair was reviewed in *No. 1 Magazine* in March 1985; "A huge, huge step on from *The Hurting*, *Songs From The Big Chair* takes all the loose ends from the group's last year and gels them into an album that works as an album rather than a collection of different songs slung together. Particularly impressive is the use of non-electronic instruments (the piano on 'Head Over Heels' for instance) that gives the LP an especially grand feel. Look out for the haunting 'Listen'. Apart from that it would be unwise to mention any particular track on its own, the whole being greater than the sum of all parts. A triumph."

Orzabal was quoted in the *Shropshire Star* in January 2018; "I think we were probably too young to truly appreciate it. We were still growing up. And now that we're older, we appreciate everything way more. There seems to be more time nowadays. I think we are better musicians and better singers too. I kind of thank the eighteen and nineteen year old Roland for being so devoted. I didn't really know what legacy our music would create... It's just incredible when people sing back at me, you get this feeling like 'okay, if my life stopped now, it would all have been worth it'... The only thing I would have changed is that after *Songs From The Big Chair*, we toured the world for so long that it broke us. So I think if I had been the manager, I would have cut the tour in half and got us back into the studio while we were really, really relevant. Maybe, an album between *Songs From The Big Chair* and *The Seeds Of Love* would have been good."

In *The Quietus* feature of September 2013 Orzabal said; "I ended up doing primal therapy after *Songs From The Big Chair* and during *The Seeds Of Love*, and then I realised so much of you is your character, and you're born like it. I think that definitely any trauma — whether it's childhood or later in life — affects you negatively, especially when it's suppressed, but there's so much of us which is already in place. I believe that primal theory — which has been absorbed into modern psychotherapy practices — is very, very valid, but a good therapist is a good therapist. He doesn't have to be a primal therapist."

Dr Mark Griffiths, a behavioural psychologist at Nottingham Trent University, has advocated that in the context of pop music, Tears For Fears is "the most psychologically influenced band."

Orzabal was quoted in *The Guardian* in December 2013; "'Mad World''s chorus — 'The dreams in which I'm dying are the best I've ever had' — is from Janov's idea that nightmares can be good because they release tension."

Orzabal was quoted in *Super Deluxe Edition* in March 2020; "I was very much into Arthur Janov and *The Primal Scream*. I remember going out for a meal with Ian Stanley and his girlfriend and my wife at the time. And he said to me, 'do you know how much money you've made?' And I didn't really care because I wanted to do primal therapy, because that's the kind of guy I was. And that's what I did, and clearly it was the most important thing to me at that time."

On meeting Arthur Janov, Orzabal said; "We broke it really big with *Songs From The Big Chair*, both in England and America, and then he became hyper-aware of who we were. So we were doing four nights at Hammersmith Odeon, and he came to one of them. We met in the dressing room afterwards. I spoke to him a couple of times on the phone, and we all met up for lunch — me, Curt and our partners — in some fancy restaurant in Chelsea."

Smith said; "(Janov) proceeded to ask us whether we might be interested in writing a musical about primal theory. At that point I lost the plot... Basically it was as if God had come down and said that he wanted you to find ways to make him money. It would be like God taking sponsorship... I don't think lyrics were his (Janov's) strong point! You know, there are some words you don't put in songs, and long psychological explanations are really not things that songs are written about! I was destroyed after meeting Arthur Janov."

Smith was quoted in *Radio Television Luxemburg* in June 2019; "Primal theory really concentrated on moving through traumatic experiences to exorcise those demons, but I don't think I'm exorcising demons now, as far as music goes. I think if anything, you're putting yourself back to a time when you were more innocent, which is also a good thing. I mean music is a kind of therapy no matter which way you look at it, both for those listening and those playing, and you have to embrace that part of it."

It is inspirational that when Orzabal and Smith opted to use music as therapy by expressing events and pains in their life through song, it captured the imagination of many others. Smith said in *Medium* in January 2020; "I don't think I ever looked for music that "lifted me up", I was always attracted to music that made me feel like I belonged. That other people felt the same way as me. Be that punk, the ska resurgence or in later years Peter Gabriel, Bowie and Talking Heads. It was about finding music that I felt I could relate to and more importantly, the feeling that they related to me... I don't think I've ever managed to channel pure happiness into a song. When I feel that way, which is often, I'm embracing the moment and don't feel the need to write. It's normally when I'm trying to work things out that I write and the songs can turn out positive or negative depending on the outcome."

There is perhaps something very cathartic in that. In particular, with the subject of teenage angst explored liberally in *The Hurting*, it has been popular over the years among younger listeners. In *Vice* in January 2014 Smith said; "I think people in their late teens and early twenties tend to relate to the album more than any other age group because they're just finding themselves. They've just left home and are dealing with not having that family support anymore. For us, we never had the family support so it made no difference."

He was quoted in *Billboard* in November 2017; "We are finding, specifically with Spotify, that we are garnering a younger audience of people that are actually discovering *The Hurting* and *Songs from The Big Chair*, the latter, weirdly, to a lesser degree, which is surprising because *The Hurting* wasn't a big hit, except for in Los Angeles and New York, but *The Hurting* is the one they gravitate towards... as far as the younger audience goes, that that's the age we were at when we wrote it. I think it's a younger audience that relates to the lyrical content more than anything else."

Orzábal told *The Guardian*; "'Mad World' hasn't dated because it's expressive of a period I call the teenage menopause, where your hormones are going crazy as you're leaving childhood. Your fingers are on the cliff and you're about to drop off, but somehow you cling on."

Smith; "We've had people like MGMT coming to shows in Detroit; Foster The People when we were in Korea; younger bands that really cite *The Hurting* as a big influence. And you meet other people, like Billy Corgan or Gwen Stefani, who are beside themselves because they were such big fans when they were younger. You might say it's juvenile, or depression, or angst, but it seems that a lot of people go through that phase. And it stretches across the age spectrum, which is interesting. And genres as well. I mean, Swiss Beatz is a big fan. Hardcore rap groups like Gangstarr. Kanye West sampled 'Memories Fade' on his album. He hadn't sought permission for it. One side of you is pissed because he thinks it's his song because he changed the lyric. He kept the melody, he sampled the track. That's Kanye West for you! But the people that cite us as influences or sample our tracks, it's a compliment. I prefer to take it that way."

Smith said in *Medium* in January 2020; "I honestly don't think it's any different today than it was when we were coming up through the industry. For us it was 'where's the single that radio will play?' and now it's 'how do we get the streams/ clicks?' The artists that will last are those that make complete bodies of work like The 1975, Bon Iver and Phoebe Bridgers."

Particularly in the early days of their career, many of Tears For Fears' promotional appearances were in teen magazines and youth oriented TV. By the early eighties, there was pretty much a universal understanding that pop music relied strongly on style and image; essentially, it could be considered that an element of being willing to "dumb down" was required to play the game. It raises the question as to whether it might have been frustrating for any group who were more interested in music than image. It's ironic to think that with the musical and emotional depth of *The Hurting* being what it is, Tears For Fears were possibly still part of a media machine that were so willing to merge them as another "boy band".

On having attracted a young fanbase, Orzabal told *New Musical Express* in November 1982; "I can understand that to an extent with Curt being the pin-up, but records don't sell purely because of that. People are ultimately attracted to the music — there are loads of good-looking people around who are doing nothing. Our music is the thing that's getting to people. I don't think the kids really understand the magnitude of what we're talking about."

He told *Melody Maker* in March the following year; "The

press have a go at us, saying 'you're just a bunch of pretty faces!' I mean, fucking hell, *look* at us!" To which Smith retorted, "We've got bleeding bags under our eyes!"

Equally though, it is important not to attempt to elevate any music above the other; who's to say that the more commercially compatible music is less deserving or of lower quality? It's incredibly subjective. On such basis, whilst it would be easy to assess that Tears For Fears were putting above average music on the table in the early eighties, it is important to acknowledge that what they did was of its time; *The Hurting* fitted in with the musical style at the time although on balance, it wasn't without its uniqueness.

It was advocated in *New Musical Express* in November 1982; "Tears For Fears can compete with the chart's own superficial level but they also possess the bonus of a depth of material that should ensure significant album sales across the board — from dewy eyed teenagers and bedsitter dwellers alike."

Upon being asked, "Was it ever frustrating to deliver such thought-provoking songs and complex music, and yet be treated in some media as another "boy band" with distinct hairstyles, and so forth?" Smith told *Medium* in January 2020: "To a certain degree yes, but I don't believe we've ever over thought it. The joy of being separate (not above) the fray is that we were singularly focused on what we were doing and not influenced by critics and journalists. Everyone has an opinion but an artist has to be confident in their own."

Smith told *The Quietus*, "Obviously we had a dark side, and back then I got the comparisons to Joy Division and New Order, but we'd never really seen ourselves as a genre/act, the reason being both of us are incredibly unconscious of fashion. When there's a genre of music there's a fashion that goes with it, normally, and I don't think we fit into that because we were from Bath and most of the genres were city based. They were

Manchester, or they were London. We were from a small town, so I don't think we ever felt like we fitted in with anything particularly."

Orzabal added: "The thing that set us out from the crowd, I think, was that we were quite happy to take on slightly more semi-intellectual concepts, you know, and try and turn them into hits. We were young, weren't we? And relatively handsome! In chunky knitwear!"

In Tears For Fears' early days, there is a possibility that there was a disparity between what they wanted to do creatively and what they were being urged to do commercially. *New Musical Express* reported in November 1982; "Tears For Fears are in a quandary. Thrust into the limelight by a record buying public seeming more avaricious for more pretty faces and pretty tunes every week, they hardly seem prepared for the treadmill they're already on. Despite Roland's wish to 'avoid being like other bands', it'll take strong wills to avoid the pressure that increases with every upward chart shift. There are already fights with Phonogram about follow-ups. Although a re-issue of 'Pale Shelter', their fine, neglected second single, would seem the obvious move, Phonogram, urging a rapid release (Christmas time spelling much mazooma), are tussling with the boys, who prefer to wait until a superior cut is complete."

Orzabal's response was: "So many groups are purely exploitative once they've had hits. The more you go on the more you trust your own opinion. We have to decide what do we want to hear in the charts."

Smith told *Record Mirror* in February 1983: "We've got ideas of what we want things to be like. It's not necessarily "making it" but getting things to a stage where everything goes the way we want it. I mean we're still slightly confused in our direction. We're dithering about with certain things. The next album will have a definite direction. I'll be pleased when I think we're much better musically — we don't have to reach a degree of commercial success at all."

To which the interviewer asked, "Oh, come now, surely you need to sell records to simply keep working." To which Orzabal responded, "Our attitude has changed since 'Mad World'. It's changed almost as a matter of course. Also I don't think it's a bad thing because we're in a position to reach far more people than before."

Smith: "There's a business side. We use it. We don't do it because we enjoy it — we realise it's necessary."

"We were locked away in this penthouse studio in Abbey Road, cut away from everything, for nearly a year. I think it took its toll," said Smith in 2013. "The hours were long, and it was back then when we were young. In later years in life you learn that anything you do after midnight is worthless because you're just too tired. You think something's good and then you come back in the next day and you realise it was dreadful. And there was the pressure from the record company. We realised we had something with 'Mad World', and we needed more than one hit from an album. I guess being tugged in every direction did make it hard. Plus then we got management, so there's another voice in your ear. It's the pressure of the business, the side that myself and Roland have never enjoyed that much."

Chris Hughes added, "There was pressure there. There were late nights, but there were tracks we were making that were extremely well received. I had no interest in rushing and not giving due care and attention to things. We weren't trying to capture a first take punk outburst."

Smith: "It definitely got harder after 'Mad World'. We didn't want to make just a commercial album. We wanted to make a statement. I think we were quite pretentious. That was the age we were at. We were convinced that we were right in everything we did. Show me a twenty-year-old college student or university student who's not pretentious. That's what you are at that age. You think you know everything. It's not till later on in life you realise you don't. And that was all part and parcel of what we did. We were not a one-dimensional band. Songs like 'Ideas As Opiates' and 'The Prisoner' were definitely the side that, in a weird way, during the recording became more important to get across."

In November 1983, Tears For Fears released their sixth single, 'The Way You Are'. It was their fourth single in a row to become a top forty hit. The single was intended to fill the gap between the release of *The Hurting* and what would become the band's second album, *Songs From The Big Chair*. The song was basically intended as a means of keeping Tears For Fears visible in the public eye at a time when pop music was fast changing and growing to be all the more manufactured.

Orzabal was quoted of the period that followed the success of *The Hurting* in *Super Deluxe Edition* in March 2020; "We were transitioning and transitions are notoriously difficult because you don't know where you are in that process. We knew we were getting somewhere else, going somewhere else, but we didn't quite know where. It was daunting, but we were constantly working and there was never a sense that there was no light at the end of the tunnel."

Did Tears For Fears experience a sense of disillusionment after the success of *The Hurting?* Well, possibly. Orzabal was quoted in 2013; "By the time we got to twenty one we'd become professional musicians. It became a job. After that it just became more and more watered down and more mainstream. And that's a fact. It's just the way it ended up."

'The Way You Are' is the only Tears For Fears song that was written by the full band, including Ian Stanley and Manny Elias. The song was written whilst they were on tour promoting *The Hurting*. It made full use of sampled voices and rhythms — symptomatic of the ever-growing trend in new wave music at the time.

Curt Smith did the lead vocals on 'The Way You Are'.

The B-side of the single was a track called 'The Marauders'. Although the song did reasonably well commercially, Tears For Fears were not particularly happy with 'The Way You Are', so much so that the song wasn't included on *Songs From The Big Chair* or even, Tears For Fears' 1992 *Greatest Hits* album. It was eventually included on the 1999 release of *The Hurting*.

Orzabal was quoted in *Super Deluxe Edition* in March 2020; "I continued to write on my own and the collaborations with *Songs From The Big Chair* happened after my writing sessions. So, I would have songs without a middle eight, or songs without a verse. And that's when Ian and Chris forced the issue, with pure creativity and it was blatantly obvious that their arrangements, productions and finishing of the song were superb."

In 1984, Tears For Fears decided that they would stop using recording studios and work from Ian Stanley's home studio instead. The latter had always been a preferable place to work from because the environment was more relaxed with no time pressures. Good idea. It was at Stanley's place that the material for *Songs From The Big Chair* was written.

Songs From The Big Chair is demonstrative that after *The Hurting*, Tears For Fears were creating a more commercial sound. Bolstered by the singles 'Shout' and 'Everybody Wants To Rule The World', 1985 signified the turning point at which Smith and Orzabal became internationally famous popstars.

Orzabal was quoted in *Super Deluxe Edition* in March 2020; "We'd already scored with some hits from *The Hurting*. And (Dave Bates) attitude was, 'you've got a song, we're putting it out as a single. It sounds like a single, we're putting it out.' He was constantly keeping us in the market, and it was through that single ('Mother's Talk') that we got to 'Shout'. And then we go to 'Everybody Wants To Rule The World'."

It was considered in *Rolling Stone* in June 1985; "As Tears For Fears, Smith and Orzabal, both twenty three, have since turned their primal screaming into a successful new wave act. The pair's 1983 debut album, *The Hurting*, topped a million in world sales and spawned three top five singles in England. Their latest LP, *Songs From The Big Chair*, could beat that. 'Shout' has already been a major common market hit, while in America, 'Everybody Wants To Rule The World', a sober synth-bop number with a catchy chorus and a surprising heavy-metal guitar solo, has cracked the top twenty... They exchanged the brooding tone of 'Mad World' and 'Pale Shelter' on *The Hurting* for the more commercial sound of *Songs From The Big Chair*."

Tears For Fears might well have felt the need to distance themselves from *The Hurting* by the time it came to promoting their second album. It was considered in *Radio & Records* in August 1985; "Tears For Fears' determination to counter their image extends to the official bio — an unlikely place for analysis — which insists 'there's a redemptive pop accessibility to their music and a subtle underlying optimism to their worldview'... The death-is-the-only-relief bent of their lyrics stemmed from the primal scream theories of Arthur Janov. Tears For Fears is now beginning to inch away from that image."

In the same feature Orzabal was quoted; "It's very hard explaining someone else's theories. I can agree with Janov wholeheartedly, but I still can't put it across. It probably did backfire, take away from our trying to be our true selves."

In September 1985, *Musician* advocated that *Songs From The Big Chair* was "a significant advance over *The Hurting*: bigger and stronger in all ways, and considerably more cheerful, for all the continued intensity of its lyrical content."

Songs From The Big Chair was reviewed in *Rolling Stone* in May 1985; "Tears For Fears sounds a lot like a lot of other British bands. On the group's second album you can hear U2's social conscience, the Bunnymen's echoing guitars and XTC's contorted pop wit, as well as lead singer Curt Smith's version of the affected sob that's run through art rock from Yes to Spandau Ballet. Apparently, these elements have not been borrowed consciously but absorbed naturally — which is worse: they can't help it if you've heard it all before. What nudges *Songs From The Big Chair* slightly ahead of the pack is the sparkling production by Chris Hughes, which aspires to and sometimes achieves the chilly grandeur of Thomas Dolby's studio work. The songs inevitably progress toward dense noise, but they always begin with pristine snatches of odd hooks juxtaposed to suggest spaciousness and atmosphere. The gorgeous saxophone and bell-like electric keyboards that precede the Latin rhythms of 'The Working Hour', for instance, conjure a daydream of heaven to distract the workingman from his woes. Except for 'Everybody Wants To Rule The World', a catchy Beatlesque number updated to the Synth Age, the songs are more interesting for their textures than for their melodies or lyrics. The last cut, 'Listen', has the most to offer in terms of sheer beauty, with its cracking-glacier sound effects and airy synths, wafting operatic soprano and inscrutable chanting. It leaves only an elusive impression, but it's a lovely surprise at the end of an album typified by crunch rockers like 'Shout' and 'Broken'."

"We were going off to countries we'd never been to before, so it was kind of exciting as well for us," recalled Smith in 2013. "It was very tiring, there was little spare time, but we were young and we were seeing new places, and so there's a certain excitement about that. I did find the screaming girls a bit peculiar. That's just the way we were. We were undoubtedly awkward. It was peculiar for people like us to experience people trying to rip your clothing off. In England it was a big number one record. It went straight to number one as soon as it came out. It was sort of a big cult hit in America."

Orzabal was quoted in *Super Deluxe Edition* in March 2020; "At the time *Songs From The Big Chair* felt completely disjointed, that we were clutching at straws regarding available songs. We started off with two or three songs and bits of B-sides and within one month I came up with 'Shout', 'Everybody Wants To Rule The World', and 'I Believe'. And I think it was when we did 'Shout' that we really moved to a completely different gear. One of the reasons it was called *Songs From The Big Chair*, I probably told you this a million times, is that it felt disparate; it wasn't like *The Hurting* which was almost like a life work for us. Albeit we were teenagers. Hence the title *Songs* because it just seemed to me like eight separate songs, and even the track 'Listen' was an Ian Stanley (keyboard player) demo and made while we were recording *The Hurting*. But I don't know why, I think it was possibly the fact that we'd done our initial first demos in Ian's house in Bath. And then he won a little bit of money from the publishing, we built the studio there in a bigger room, in his house. And I think it was almost like coming back to the West Country and even Chris Hughes had links to Bath, because his mum lived there. So, I think getting out of the huge studios and into this real intimate setting, the birthplace of Tears For Fears almost, which was Ian Stanley's house. I think that created this, you know, more of a calm but hot-housed environment. Plus, this massive input of new technology, like the Fairlight, the Synclavier and the Drumulator. We had all these cutting-edge sounds to play with and I think that the secrets are in the arrangement and production, because it really is superb."

By the late eighties, the stylistic features of pop music had changed exponentially and the sounds of choice were more in the lexicon of acid house and techno. Dance music had changed, pop music had changed, and as a result, *The Hurting* and even *Songs From The Big Chair* sounded chronically out of place to the young record buying public. As with many established rock and new wave acts, Tears For Fears were lost in the obscurity of a sea of change. In the long run though, despite the fact that the overall sound of the album is arguably dated, *The Hurting* stands up to scrutiny in terms of what its overall merits are.

The 1999 release of the album was reviewed in *Q* in July of that year: "Despite its occasional bum note, *The Hurting* remains a landmark work... a highly emotional pop record, at its simplest."

The thirtieth anniversary release of *The Hurting* was reviewed in *Mojo* in December 2013: "Has there ever been a more thoroughly miserable mainstream pop album than *The Hurting*?... Even when it is up-tempo it is sombre, and at its most musically adventurous, in the cavernous minimalism of 'Ideas As Opiates' and gnarly dissonances of 'The Prisoner', it's almost unbearably bereft... But in essence, it was pop."

It is worth checking out the 1999 and 2013 editions of *The Hurting* because it is an opportunity to hear variations on the original album, both in terms of content and sonically. Taking the bonus tracks into consideration and the way in which they offer insight and context into the original release of *The Hurting*, they are certainly worthwhile.

In their recent concerts, Tears For Fears have always included songs from *The Hurting*. Commercially sensible, as their earlier hits are what they are most known for. However, over three decades after the album was first written, both Orzabal and Smith have been very open about the fact that naturally, they are different people today compared to who they were when they made *The Hurting*. As a result, the way in which they relate to the themes of the album as musicians and as individuals has changed over the years.

Orzabal was quoted in *Vice* in January 2014; "Writing for me, when I was a young boy was extremely personal, and now it's not. I think these feelings are more prevalent in your teenage years. You find it hard to deal with certain things and as you get older it becomes easier."

Essentially, the emotions and experiences that drove them

when they made *The Hurting* are very much in the past. It is plausibly something that changes the way in which they have delivered the songs live on stage in recent years. Smith was quoted in *Vice* in January 2014; "Sometimes when you're singing some of these songs, you have to change arrangements because you don't feel the same way anymore."

Upon being asked, "How do you gear yourself to deliver an impressive, emotive performance of such poignant lyrics at each concert? Do you have to envision the anguish of childhood each time?" Smith told *Medium* in January 2020; "I certainly attempt to put myself back to that time because that is how I felt. It doesn't make the emotion any less legitimate because I don't feel that way now. I'm also aware that members of the audience may feel the way that I did and it's important that they know we evolve. Normally for the better."

Smith was quoted in *Radio Television Luxemburg* in June 2019; "When I'm singing a song I need to put myself back into the mind of that person that wrote the song, and in this case of course it's you but at a younger age so you put yourself back into the position of where you were and how you felt at that point in time, otherwise it's just not really genuine and you're just becoming a cover band. But yeah I still feel a deep connection with pretty much everything we've done."

Upon being asked "What are your thoughts today on your song 'Mad World' — is it more valid now than it was before? Smith was quoted in the same feature; "Well that's another interesting thing about singing old songs, because then you don't have to put yourself back into that situation because it is still valid now and all you're doing is thinking of different influences. They'd be the same lyrics, but if it were to be current, it would just be influenced by different people. Back then it was influenced by what was going on in the world at that point in time. Same shit different day! You know it's the same kind of stuff, only you interchange the actors involved." He was quoted in *Rolling Stone* in June 1985; "People think we're being heavy about something that, to us, is perfectly obvious."

Orzabal said in September 2013; "Most of the songs were written in the flat that I shared with Caroline, who's my wife now of thirty years. It's above a pizza restaurant now. I don't know if it was a pizza place then, but it's bang in the centre of Bath, and me being unemployed, and without anything really to do or to get up for, I used to sit at the window and just watch people go about their work. It was simple as that. Writing those songs was therapeutic, definitely. The recording of the album, not so."

Smith was quoted in *Medium* in January 2020; "There are always three distinct layers to music for me. The lyrical, the melody/song and the production. The lyrical and melodic side can move me emotionally and intellectually. The production side moves me bodily and intellectually. It's artists that manage to combine all of these facets that I tend to gravitate towards. In my early teenage years it was anger and disillusionment — Sex Pistols, Specials, UB40. In my late teens and twenties it was attempting to understand those feelings — Peter Gabriel, David Bowie etc. As I grew older I understood that holding on to my "teenage angst" was not going to benefit me emotionally, my task then was to understand it and attempt to move past it."

To date, Tears For Fears have sold more than thirty million albums worldwide. They remain respected, known and enjoyed, as does their work. In terms of how Tears For Fears are welcomed by audiences today, Orzabal was quoted in July 2019 in the *Yorkshire Times* concerning a gig they had recently done at the time: "The scale was much larger than we had ever been used to, to go back and play the O2 Arena and sell it out and have screens behind us, screens above us, to see the audience and hear the audience reaction, people who are now our age, and younger, it just felt like this huge acceptance and it's something Curt said recently that when you first start out you get acceptance, then when you're successful everyone hates you, and now finally coming back aged fifty-seven, having toured virtually every year in America, never in England, to get that welcome that we got from all the audiences was absolutely heart-warming."

Orzabal said in the *Shropshire Star* in January 2018; "We used to tour to support a record. Now touring is an industry in itself. I don't know why or when it changed. But touring is quite easy to do now."

In 2013, Lorde did a cover of 'Everybody Wants To Rule The World' and in 2003, the version of 'Mad World' by Michael Andrews and Gary Jules made some very noticeable waves. Characteristically, their version was very stripped down; in terms of instrumentation, it utilised only piano, subtle use of a vocoder on the chorus and a mellotron to imitate a cello sound. A far cry from the fully synthesised and percussive original by Tears For Fears. The Andrews and Jules version of 'Mad World' was originally released in 2002 as part of the soundtrack to the 2001 film, *Donnie Darko*. Orzabal commented on it in *Vice* in January 2014; "A friend brought over the *Donnie Darko* soundtrack and put it on before I'd even seen the film. My son was about eight at the time and he started singing the lyrics to 'Mad World'. I thought; 'Oh God, no, what have I forced upon him! I was joking, I didn't feel like that!'"

The growing popularity of the film was such that the featured version of 'Mad World' was released as a single in December 2003. Released as part of the race for the Christmas number one that year, it beat The Darkness' song, 'Christmas Time (Don't Let The Bells End)' to the top spot.

Smith commented in 2013; "The subject matter seemed to click with people. How simple it was, and how dark it was, seemed to connect. It says something about the English psyche, that's for sure, as did the Gary Jules version being a number one hit at Christmas. That's hardly the subject matter one would consider for a Christmas hit! And ours got to number three over the Christmas period as well. Maybe English people get depressed over Christmas."

Orzabal said in *The Guardian* in December 2013; "Two decades later, Gary Jules sang 'Mad World' for the film *Donnie Darko* and got the Christmas number one in 2003. That was probably the proudest moment of my career. I was in my forties and had forgotten how I felt when I wrote all those Tears For Fears songs. I thought, 'thank God for the nineteen-year-old Roland Orzabal. Thank God he got depressed'."

The Andrews and Jules version of 'Mad World' came about when the director of *Donnie Darko*, Richard Kelly, commissioned San Diego musician Michael Andrews to work on the soundtrack for the film. Andrews already had a strong portfolio having already composed for film and television as well as having been in several bands — The Greyboy Allstars, and The Origin, of which he was in with Gary Jules. As a soundtrack composer, Andrews was inspired by John Barry and Ennio Morricone and in such vein, he wanted to include a song as part of his otherwise instrumental score. With Tears For Fears being one of Andrews' favourite childhood bands, he decided that 'Mad World' would be a fitting choice of song for the film.

Andrews played the piano on the song and he invited Jules to provide vocals. After ninety minutes working together, they had the whole song recorded. Although *Donnie Darko* was a critically acclaimed film, it wasn't a strong commercial success. That said, it sold well on home release and it is regarded as a film with cult status. All of which contributed as a catalyst to the Andrews and Jules cover of 'Mad World' getting the recognition it deserved. Jules advocated that the song was easy for people to relate to. He was quoted in *BBC News* in December 2003; "I think it's a really beautiful example of a person struggling with the fact that life is mad. I honestly think it's one of the most beautiful songs I have ever heard and the way it's stripped down now just pins people… Every so often a song with just vocals, piano and cello creeps up on you and says something about who you are, where you're going which stops you in your tracks."

The Darkness' single was actually the UK bookmakers' favourite to get the Christmas 2003 number one spot but when 'Mad World' beat it, the latter stayed at number one in the UK singles chart for three solid weeks. However, the song's success in the US was not parallel to what it had achieved in the UK.

In 2006, the Andrews and Jules version of 'Mad World' was included in the commercial for the video game, *Gears Of War*. It once again resulted in the song moving up the charts. A performance of 'Mad World' by Adam Lambert on the eighth season of American Idol also briefly garnered interest and boosted its sales. Gary Jules performed 'Mad World' with Mylène Farmer as part of her Timeless tour in 2013.

The amount of time that has gone by since the release of *The Hurting* has highlighted its significance. Because it was Tears For Fears' debut album, it is argued by some that their ideas and musical execution of them were not as fully formed and developed as they came to be on their second album, *Songs From The Big Chair*. It is an interesting perspective in terms of how — as with any artist in any art form — with time often comes improvement.

However, it would seem excessive to use the differences in commercial success between *Songs From The Big Chair* and *The Hurting* as a scale to indicate quality, relevance or significance. Basically, although *Songs From The Big Chair* was more commercially rewarding for Tear For Fears, it's not to say that *The Hurting* is any less important in terms of Tears For Fears' legacy and indeed, as an excellent album in its own right.

Orzabal was quoted in *The Sun* in November 2017; "I think

it's down to the lyrics. We were brave enough to tackle certain subjects that maybe other bands at the time wouldn't have a clue about. A song about post-teenage angst like 'Mad World' seems to be permanently relevant."

At the time, there was a sense that Tears For Fears were less pleased with their second album then they were with the sound they initially had on *The Hurting*. Orzabal was quoted in *Rolling Stone* in June 1985; "What Americans are getting at the moment, is watered-down Tears For Fears."

Regarding the chorus of 'Shout', he was quoted in the same feature; "I thought it was too simple, a bit crass." Years later though, Orzabal was quoted in *Classic Pop Mag* in May 2020; "Songwriting is about how open you are and, when you're younger, you're naturally more open. I had a month off and was putting a lot of rhythms of songs I loved into the Linn Drum machine. One of those was Talking Heads'. It was that rhythm, plus me and a Prophet synthesiser in a big echoey room. I went into a semi-hypnotic state and 'Shout' just popped in from the ether. It was the turning point, because 'Shout' has what were familiar motifs from our earlier songs, but it was *The Hurting* growing up."

In response to the question, "Is it true that you weren't keen on 'Everybody Wants To Rule The World' at first?" Orzabal was quoted in the same feature; "Yeah. It was another song from the experience of putting great rhythms into the Linn Drum machine, this time Simple Minds' 'Waterfront' and 'Throw Away The Key' by Linx. The problem was, I didn't have the lyric. It was originally called 'Everybody Wants To Go To War', which I knew didn't work. My wife Caroline loved it but, when you're a songwriter who doesn't like the lyric, the song dies. It was our producer Chris Hughes who championed 'Everybody Wants To Rule The World'. It got to the point where, at 6pm at the end of every session, he'd make us spend an hour going over and over it. That's where I came up with the guitar figure and changing it to '...Rule The World', which is when I thought, 'Yeah, that's good'."

Orzabal was quoted of 'Everybody Wants To Rule The World' in *Super Deluxe Edition* in March 2020; "I mean that track has just got a life of its own. It's crazy, I mean, it was always popular, but then... I did an interview with Reuters or something like that, a while back, with this lady who went on Spotify and worked out that there are about one hundred and forty cover versions of that song; I mean, from Don Henley to Patti Smith, to Weezer, to Lorde, obviously. It's crazy, it's one of those songs, isn't it? I remember from my childhood, there'd be songs like 'Lola' by The Kinks, it just, you know, it's always going to be around; it's a classic. I don't get it and I didn't get it at the time, I mean, I think it was the way that Chris made us improvise it every day, after our recording session, I would get on the guitar and Ian would get on the keyboards, Chris would be on the Fairlight and it soon became effortless. Every time we'd push up the faders, even if they were out of balance — because you didn't have total recall back then, and nothing like we have nowadays with computers, Pro Tools and Logic — every time we pushed them up it was just, 'wow'. There's something intrinsic to it, you know, it's just, it's got a magic quality and so damn bloody simple. But yeah, in some ways there's only one real Tears For Fears album and that was *The Hurting*. Because we went off script pretty much straight away, the moment we moved out of making personal statements to almost semi-political statements and then with *The Seeds Of Love*, very political statements, but yeah, I'll take it, though. I'm happy."

On balance, there is a sense that Tears For Fears have always been rather self critical. Not long after the release of *The Hurting*, they were candid about parts of it that they were not happy with at the time. Orzabal was quoted in *Melody Maker* in March 1983; "For us, the first side is half of a perfect album. We couldn't get the same effect on the second side and we admit that. We think we've made half of a great album. I think that on the first album we've lost a lot of the guts and emotion that we started out with, because of the labour of it. It was virtually, almost traumatic, the whole experience… We'll never be prolific, because we're fussy."

In response to the fact that by the time of the interview, Tears For Fears had put out three versions of 'Pale Shelter', two versions of 'Ideas As Opiates' and three versions of 'Change', Smith said, "If we've recorded a song and it's not that good, and then we re-record it and we then think it's really good, we believe we should release it for people to hear."

Is there still pressure today on Tears For Fears to live up to the success of their previous work? Well, perhaps not. Smith was quoted in *Radio Television Luxemburg* in June 2019; "What you've done in the past is going to influence what you're doing now, but I don't think we really think about it when we go to a studio. Normally when we record it's just about trying to make the best that we can do at that point in time. We're not really looking for influences or anything else, it's about what feels right, but in general it's always going to end up sounding like us, because it *is* us."

It comes across that the whole fame game might not have been Tears For Fears' cup of tea. Orzabal was quoted in *Record Mirror* in November 1982; "I don't have any hobbies. I like staying in a lot with Caroline. We don't do anything, we don't watch television — or not much. If I do go out, we like going out to eat. Eating is one of my greatest pleasures. There are plenty of good restaurants in Bath and quite a few decent clubs as well. Moles is my favourite because it has a very relaxed atmosphere, not at all posey. I don't read as a rule, and when I do it's never fiction. I like psychology books and things to do with science, and the physiology of the body."

He was quoted in *Record Mirror* in February 1983; "Bath's

really great. I don't like being reminded that I'm in Tears For Fears all the time. Bath is a good way of getting away from it."

The *Sunday Mirror* reported in March 1985; "Tears For Fears singer Curt Smith nearly had a breakdown and quit the pop scene last year. The twenty-three-year-old star, whose band is at number one with 'Everybody Wants To Rule The World', felt desperately depressed and uninspired. But he was pulled back from the brink by the most important person in his life — his lovely wife Lynne Altman... Lynne's powers of persuasion have paid handsome dividends. Since those dark days, Curt and his Tears For Fears partner Roland Orzabal have produced their platinum album, *Songs From The Big Chair*. Curt happily admits he owes his success to Lynne... Marriage has helped Curt calm down."

In the same feature Smith continued; "I would have gladly left the pop world forever. I was very tempted to go back to my old job as a teacher... Before I met her (Lynne) I desperately craved for love and affection, and did lots of stupid things to draw attention to myself. The silliest thing I did was several years ago when I broke into my school — Beecham Cliff Comprehensive at Bath — and stole cameras. I was later done for burglary after the man in the camera shop recognised me when I tried to sell them... (Lynne) went out to work every day and brought home a wage packet to support us both. The happiest day in my life was at Christmas when I told her to quit the job and promised to support her for the rest of our lives together. Lynne is far more important to me than success, and I would never dream of leaving her for anyone else. But she knows this, and totally trusts me when I'm away. We have the most wonderful home and we wouldn't swap it for London, or anywhere else in the world."

With time, comes new perspectives and new relationships. Smith was quoted in *The Sun* in November 2017; "I have no regrets. The healthiest thing I did was to leave and move to

America. I hated the invasion of my personal life back then. And I hated being surrounded by a bunch of enablers who were making money from you. To preserve my sanity I had to leave England and move to New York. Then I met my wife, Frances, and we've been together thirty years now. New York was a fantastic place to disappear because no one cares who you are. No one bothers you. In my ten years living there I was never once asked for an autograph or stopped on the street. It was an absolute joy. I gave myself time and space to get to know myself more."

Regarding his experiences when *Songs From The Big Chair* took off in the States, Orzabal was quoted in *Classic Pop Mag* in May 2020; "I'd never left my home country. It was a massive adventure, travelling for the first time, where everyone thinks you're special on two levels: you're a successful musical act and you're English. The American music scene was a notoriously closed shop, but every now and again it opens up and we just got lucky, because we came in on a wave of British bands with the right material. It was hard graft, but there was a magical feeling going to crazy places like Nashville, New Orleans and Biloxi."

The Hurting was successful amongst a range of eclectic musical styles in 1983 and by 1985, Tears For Fears were still up against some similar challenges prior to *Songs From The Big Chair* taking off commercially.

Orzabal was quoted of 'Shout' in *Super Deluxe Edition* in March 2020; "Yeah, it was very much in the Tears For Fears theme, based on *The Hurting*. Not a lot of people know this, obviously it was a big hit at Christmas, but behind the scenes there was a bit of a struggle to get that traction on the radio, probably because of 'The Way You Are' and 'Mother's Talk'. Dave had to do his very best bullying, I think, to make sure that it took off. Once we had it on MTV and once we did *Top Of The Pops*, it started to fly. But it could've been a completely different story if Dave hadn't been so stubborn... It was a chock-a-block chart. I mean, you had Band Aid and Paul McCartney's Frog Chorus ('We All Stand Together'), 'Last Christmas' from Wham!, you know, those were the songs keeping us off the top spot. All excellent works, in and of themselves."

By combining the exploration of lyrics inspired by the psychology of Arthur Janov and some damn good melody, instrumentation and structure, Tears For Fears put out an important piece of work in 1983. Of course, *The Hurting* does sound dated in terms of the instrumentation used; there is no getting away from that and it is noticeable from the very start of the album right through to the very end of it. But musically, does this make *The Hurting* any less valuable? I would argue that it doesn't.

Also, whether or not *The Hurting* sounds dated musically is irrelevant in terms of how a key part of its legacy is in how emotionally unreserved it is. Smith was quoted of *The Hurting* in *Vice* in January 2014; "I'm very proud of it. It doesn't beat around the bush. It's not being subtle in any way so in that sense it's probably the purest Tears For Fears record."

Pop music in the eighties was plastered with synths, sampling and boy bands with eccentric haircuts. Thirty years later though, there is no denying that *The Hurting* stands out, and for all the right reasons.

The Hurting
A Comprehensive Discography

Album Personnel

Tears For Fears
Roland Orzabal - lead vocals and backing vocals, guitars, keyboards, rhythm programming
Curt Smith - lead vocals and backing vocals, bass, keyboards
Manny Elias - drums, rhythm programming
Ian Stanley - keyboards programming, computer programming

Additional personnel
Chris Hughes - rhythm programming, tunes percussion, conducting
Ross Cullum - jazz high, dynamic toggle (percussion)
Mel Collins - saxophones
Phil Palmer - Palmer picking (guitar)
Caroline Orzabal - child vocal on 'Suffer The Children'

Production
Chris Hughes
Ross Cullum

Track Listing

All songs written by Roland Orzabal unless noted.

Original release
Side One
1. 'The Hurting' (4:20)
2. 'Mad World' (3:35)
3. 'Pale Shelter' (4:34)
4. 'Ideas As Opiates' (3:46)
5. 'Memories Fade' (5:08)

Side Two
6. 'Suffer The Children' (3:53)
7. 'Watch Me Bleed' (4:18)
8. 'Change' (4:15)
9. 'The Prisoner' (2:55)
10. 'Start Of The Breakdown' (5:00)

Cassette only bonus track
11. 'Change' (New Version) (4:36)

1999 remastered and expanded edition additional tracks
11. 'Pale Shelter (Long Version)' (7:09) *
12. 'The Way You Are (Extended)' (7:43) **
13. 'Mad World (World Remix)' (3:42)
14. 'Change (Extended Version)' (6:00)

Notes
*The 1999 remastered version of the album incorrectly credits Curt Smith as co-writer and Mike Howlett as producer of 'Pale Shelter" (Long Version)'. As confirmed on the original releases, Smith did not write any of the tracks for *The Hurting* and this version of 'Pale Shelter' is actually the 1983 12" extended

version of the song, which was produced by Chris Hughes and Ross Cullum. Howlett produced the original 1982 version.

**'The Way You Are' was originally a non-album track, though the 12" version was included on the remastered version of *The Hurting* in 1999.

30th anniversary editions (2013)
Two deluxe editions of the album were released in October 2013. One is a double CD comprising CDs 1 and 2 (as below), and the other is a 4-disc box set comprising CDs 1–3 and a DVD (as below), a book containing interviews, a new essay from Paul Sinclair about the album, a replica of a 1983 tour programme, a discography and photos. The first five hundred pre-orders from the Universal Music online store also included a vinyl 7" single of 'Change' in a rare earlier picture sleeve.

Disc one: Original Album
1. 'The Hurting' (4:16)
2. 'Mad World' (3:35)
3. 'Pale Shelter (1983 Single Version)' (4:24)
4. 'Ideas As Opiates' (3:46)
5. 'Memories Fade' (5:01)
6. 'Suffer The Children' (3:49)
7. 'Watch Me Bleed' (4:15)
8. 'Change' (4:13)
9. 'The Prisoner' (2:55)
10. 'Start Of The Breakdown' (4:57)

Disc two: Singles and B-Sides
1. 'Suffer The Children (Original Version)' (3:40)
2. 'Pale Shelter (Original Version)' (4:39)
3. 'The Prisoner (Original 7' Version)' (2:43)
4. 'Ideas As Opiates (Alternate Version)'* (3:53)
5. 'Change (New Version)' (4:36)

6. 'Suffer The Children (Remix)' (4:15)
7. 'Pale Shelter (Long Version)' (7:09)
8. 'Mad World (World Remix)' (3:39)
9. 'Change (Extended Version)' (5:59)
10. 'Pale Shelter (New Extended Version)' (6:44)
11. 'Suffer the Children (Instrumental)' (4:26)
12. 'Change (Radio Edit)' (3:58)
13. 'Wino' (2:23)
14. 'The Conflict' (4:02)
15. 'We Are Broken'** (4:03)
16. 'Suffer the Children (Demo)' (4:04)

Notes
*Track 4, labeled as 'Ideas As Opiates (Alternate Version)', was intended to be the first version of the song (originally released as the B-Side to 'Mad World') but was mistakenly replaced by a previously unreleased version of the album track.
**Track 15, although labeled as 'We Are Broken', is actually 'Broken Revisited' which is a slightly extended version of the original track and was first included as a bonus track on the limited edition cassette of *Songs From The Big Chair* in 1985 and later included on the 1999 remastered edition and 2006 deluxe edition of the same album.

Disc three: Radio Sessions and Live
1. 'Ideas As Opiates (Peel Session 1/9/1982)' (3:48)
2. 'Suffer The Children (Peel Session 1/9/1982)' (4:03)
3. 'The Prisoner (Peel Session 1/9/1982)' (2:50)
4. 'The Hurting (Peel Session 1/9/1982)' (3:45)
5. 'Memories Fade (David Jensen BBC Session 20/10/1982)' (4:56)
6. 'The Prisoner (David Jensen BBC Session 20/10/1982)' (2:49)
7. 'Start Of The Breakdown (David Jensen BBC Session

20/10/1982)' (4:00)

8. 'The Hurting (David Jensen BBC Session 20/10/1982)' (3:50)

9. 'Start Of The Breakdown (Live at Oxford Apollo 8/4/1983)' (5:56)

10. 'Change (Live)' 4:00

DVD: *In My Mind's Eye: Live At Hammersmith Odeon (December 1983)*

1. 'Start Of The Breakdown' (6:14)
2. 'Mother's Talk' (3:50)
3. 'Pale Shelter' (4:35)
4. 'The Working Hour' (6:29)
5. 'The Prisoner' (2:52)
6. 'Ideas As Opiates' (3:43)
7. 'Mad World' (3:36)
8. 'We Are Broken' (2:57)
9. 'Head Over Heels' (4:49)
10. 'Suffer The Children' (4:02)
11. 'The Hurting' (4:24)
12. 'Memories Fade' (4:51)
13. 'Change' (4:10)

Country By Country

This list includes all releases for the main territories of UK, USA, Japan and Germany. Canadian releases by and large mirrored US ones and other European countries generally mirrored Germany.

UK
Original 11th March 1983 releases:
Mercury MERSG 17, LP*
*Limited edition with gatefold sleeve.
Mercury MERS 17, LP
Mercury MERSC 17, cassette

Reissues:
Mercury 811 039-2, 1984, CD
This was actually made in West Germany but was a universal release for Europe.

Mercury MERS 17, LP, 1985
This version came with an embossed front cover and gold foil lettering.

Universal 3743330, 3CDs / 1 DVD, 21st October 2013
Box set with 4 discs in individual card gatefold sleeves, interview booklet, and replica tour programme. Reissued on 13th March 2020.

USA
Original 11th April 1983 releases:
Mercury 811 039-1 M-1, LP
Mercury 811 039-4 M-1, cassette
Has a different cover to the UK release. It has a photo of Roland and Curt, by a lake with ducks in it. For that reason it is normally referred to as the "duck cover".

Reissues:
Mercury 811 039-2, CD, 1987
Mercury 314 558 104-2, CD, 1999*
*Remastered.

Mercury P2-11039, CD, 1992
CRC Columbia House club edition.
Mercury B0019244-02, 2CDs, October 2013
All CD releases use the UK cover.

Germany
Original 1983 releases:
Mercury 811 039-1, LP
Mercury 811 039-4, cassette
With "duck cover".

Reissues:
Mercury 811 039-2, CD, 1984
With UK cover.
Mercury 558 104-2, CD, 1999*
*Remastered.

Universal 3743330, 3CDs / 1 DVD, 18th October 2013
Box set with 4 discs in individual card gatefold sleeves, interview booklet, and
replica tour programme. Reissued on 13th March 2020.

Japan
Mercury 25PP-88, LP
"duck cover".

Mercury 28PP-1015, LP
UK cover.

Mercury 23PD-116, CD, 5th March 1989
Mercury PHCR-6102, CD, 2nd June 1993
Mercury UICY-3189, CD, 25th July 2001*
Mercury UICY-77537, CD, 4th November 2015*
*Remastered. All CDs have the UK cover.

SINGLES

There were five different singles released from the album in multiple variations and formats. This was a period in time where the record company marketing people went into overdrive. Forgive me if I have overlooked any.

UK
Suffer The Children / Wino (7")
Mercury IDEA1, 30th October 1981

Suffer The Children (remix) / Suffer The Children (instrumental) / Wino (12")
Mercury IDEA12, 30th October 1981

Suffer The Children / Wino (7")*
Mercury IDEA1, 1985

Suffer The Children (remix) / Suffer The Children (instrumental) / Wino (12")*
Mercury IDEA12, 1985
*Reissue with different sleeve.

Pale Shelter (You Don't Give Me Love) / The Prisoner (7")
Mercury IDEA2, 26th March 1982

Pale Shelter (You Don't Give Me Love) (Extended version) /
Pale Shelter (You Don't Give Me Love) / The Prisoner (12")
Mercury IDEA212, 26th March 1982

Pale Shelter (You Don't Give Me Love) / The Prisoner (7")*
Mercury IDEA2, 1985

Pale Shelter (You Don't Give Me Love) (Extended version) /
Pale Shelter (You Don't Give Me Love) / The Prisoner (12")*
Mercury IDEA212, 1985
*Reissue with different sleeve.

Mad World / Ideas As Opiates (7")
Mercury IDEA3, 24th September 1982

Mad World / Mad World (World Remix) /
Suffer The Children / Ideas As Opiates (2 x 7")
Mercury IDEA33, 30th September 1982

Mad World /
Ideas As Opiates / Saxophones As Opiates (12")
Mercury IDEA312, September 1982

Change / The Conflict (7")
Mercury IDEA 4, January 1983

Change (Extended Version) /
Change / The Conflict (7")
Mercury IDEAP 4, January 1983
Limited edition poster sleeve.

Change (Extended Version) /
Change / The Conflict (12")
Mercury IDEA 412, January 1983

Pale Shelter / We Are Broken (7")
Mercury IDEA 5, 18th April 1983

Pale Shelter / We Are Broken (7" blue vinyl)
Mercury IDEA B5, 18th April 1983

Pale Shelter / We Are Broken (7" green vinyl)
Mercury IDEA G5, 18th April 1983

Pale Shelter / We Are Broken (7" picture disc)
Mercury IDEA P5, 18th April 1983

Pale Shelter / We Are Broken (7" red vinyl)
Mercury IDEA R5, 18th April 1983

Pale Shelter / We Are Broken (7" white vinyl)
Mercury IDEA W5, 18th April 1983

**Pale Shelter (Extended Version) /
Pale Shelter / We Are Broken (12")**
Mercury IDEA 512, 18th April 1983

USA
Mad World / Ideas As Opiates (7")
Mercury 812 213-7, 1983

Change / The Conflict (7")
Mercury 812 677-7, August 1983

Germany
Mad World / Ideas As Opiates (7")
Mercury 6059 568, 1982

Mad World / Change (7")
Mercury 811 207-7, 1983

Pale Shelter / We Are Broken (7")
Mercury 812 108-7, 1983

Japan
Change / The Conflict (7")
Mercury 7PP-101, 1983

Other variations:

**Pale Shelter (Extended Version) / We Are Broken /
Mad World (World remix) / Ideas As Opiates (2 x 7")**
Vertigo SOV 2328, 1983, Canada

Tour Dates

This list features the dates of known live performances. I sourced the information from various fan websites. Where possible, I made sure to check that the information corroborated with ticket stubs and promotional posters. It is a possibility that this list is not complete.

1982

May	Moles Café, Bath, England
Friday 28th May	UMIST, Manchester, England
Saturday 29th May	Valentino's, Edinburgh, Scotland
Sunday 30th May	Maestro's, Glasgow, Scotland
Monday 31st May	Holy City Zoo, Birmingham, England
Sunday 6th June	Tiffany's, Bath, England
Thursday 16th September	Downtown, Hastings, England
Friday 17th September	Midnight Express, Bournemouth, England
Saturday 18th September	Sound Cellar, Cambridge, England
Wednesday 22nd September	Polytechnic, Manchester, England
Thursday 23rd September	Warehouse, Leeds, England
Saturday 25th September	Warehouse, Liverpool, England
Sunday 26th September	Maestros, Glasgow, Scotland

1983

Thursday 17th March	UEA, Norwich, England
Friday 18th March	Victoria Hall, Hanley, England
Saturday 19th March	Leeds University, England
Sunday 20th March	Palace, Manchester, England
Monday 21st March	Royal Court, Liverpool

Tuesday 22nd March	City Hall, Newcastle
Thursday 24th March	Capitol, Aberdeen, Scotland
Friday 25th March	Tiffany's, Glasgow, Scotland
Saturday 26th March	Lancaster University, England
Sunday 27th March	Locarno, Bristol, England
Tuesday 29th March	Top Rank, Cardiff, Wales
Wednesday 30th March	Arts Centre, Poole, England
Thursday 31st March	Queensway Hall, Dunstable, England
Saturday 2nd April	Royal Centre, Nottingham, England
Sunday 3rd April	Gaumont Theatre, Ipswich, England
Monday 4th April	Top Rank, Brighton, England
Tuesday 5th April	Winter Gardens, Margate, England
Wednesday 6th April	Civic Hall, Guildford, England
Friday 8th April	Apollo Theatre, Oxford, England
Saturday 9th April	Odeon, Birmingham, England
Sunday 10th April	Lyceum, London, England
Monday 11th April	Pavilion, Bath, England
Monday 18th April	Hammersmith Palais, London, England
Thursday 12th May	Satory-Sale, Cologne, Germany

(Broadcast on German TV show, *Rockpalast*)

Thursday 1st December	Civic Hall, Guilford, England
Friday 2nd December	UEA, Norwich, England
Saturday 3rd December	Loughborough University, England
Sunday 4th December	Royal Court, Liverpool, England
Monday 5th December	City Hall, Newcastle, England
Tuesday 6th December	Playhouse, Edinburgh, Scotland

Friday 9th December	Royal Centre, Nottingham, England
Saturday 10th December	Odeon, Birmingham, England
Sunday 11th December	Apollo, Manchester, England
Monday 12th December	Colston Hall, Bristol, England
Wednesday 14th December	Hammersmith Odeon, London, England
Thursday 15th December	Hammersmith Odeon, London, England
Friday 16th December	Winter Gardens, Margate, England
Saturday 17th December	Dome, Brighton, England
Monday 19th December	Coliseum, St. Austell, England
Tuesday 20th December	Leisure Centre, Gloucester, England
Wednesday 21st December	Guildhall, Portsmouth, England
Thursday 22nd December	Arts Centre, Poole, England

In-depth Series

The In-depth series was launched in March 2021 with four titles. Each book takes an in-depth look at an album; the history behind it; the story about its creation; the songs, as well as detailed discographies listing release variations around the world. The series will tackle albums that are considered to be classics amongst the fan bases, as well as some albums deemed to be "difficult" or controversial; shining new light on them, following reappraisal by the authors.

The first four titles published were:

Jethro Tull - Thick As A Brick	*978-1-912782-57-4*
Tears For Fears - The Hurting	*978-1-912782-58-1*
Kate Bush - The Kick Inside	*978-1-912782-59-8*
Deep Purple - Stormbringer	*978-1-912782-60-4*

Other titles in the series:

Deep Purple - Slaves And Masters
Emerson Lake & Palmer - Pictures At An Exhibition
Korn - Follow The Leader
Jethro Tull - Minstrel In The Gallery
Kate Bush - The Dreaming
Elvis Costello - This Year's Model
Deep Purple - Fireball
Talking Heads - Remain In Light
Jethro Tull - Heavy Horses
Rainbow Straight Between - The Eyes
The Stranglers - La Folie